Thomas Schirrmacher

**Leadership and Ethical Responsibility:
The Three Aspects of Every Decision**

The WEA Global Issues Series

Editors:

Bishop Efraim Tendero, Philippines
Secretary General, World Evangelical Alliance

Thomas Schirrmacher,
Director, International Institute for Religious Liberty and Speaker for Human Rights of the World Evangelical Alliance

Volumes:

1. Thomas K. Johnson – Human Rights
2. Christine Schirrmacher – The Islamic View of Major Christian Teachings
3. Thomas Schirrmacher – May a Christian Go to Court?
4. Christine Schirrmacher – Islam and Society
5. Thomas Schirrmacher – The Persecution of Christians Concerns Us All
6. Christine Schirrmacher – Islam – An Introduction
7. Thomas K. Johnson – What Difference does the Trinity Make
8. Thomas Schirrmacher – Racism
9. Christof Sauer (ed.) – Bad Urach Statement
10. Christine Schirrmacher – The Sharia: Law and Order in Islam
11. Ken Gnanakan – Responsible Stewardship of God's Creation
12. Thomas Schirrmacher – Human Trafficking
13. Thomas Schirrmacher – Ethics of Leadership
14. Thomas Schirrmacher – Fundamentalism
15. Thomas Schirrmacher – Human Rights – Promise and Reality
16. Christine Schirrmacher – Political Islam – When Faith Turns Out to Be Politics
17. Thomas Schirrmacher, Thomas K. Johnson – Creation Care and Loving our Neighbors: Studies in Environmental Ethics
18. Thomas K. Johnson (Ed.) – Global Declarations on Freedom of Religion or Belief and Human Rights

"The WEA Global Issues Series is designed to provide thoughtful, practical, and biblical insights from an Evangelical Christian perspective into some of the greatest challenges we face in the world. I trust you will find this volume enriching and helpful in your life and Kingdom service."
Bishop Efraim Tendero, Secretary General, World Evangelical Alliance

Thomas Schirrmacher

Leadership and Ethical Responsibility: The Three Aspects of Every Decision

Translator: Richard McClary
Editor: Thomas K. Johnson
Editorial Assistant: Ruth Baldwin

The WEA Global Issues Series
Volume 13

Verlag für Kultur und Wissenschaft
Culture and Science Publ.
Bonn 2017

World Evangelical Alliance
Church Street Station, P.O. Box 3402
New York, NY 10008-3402 U.S.A.
Phone +[1] 212-233-3046
Fax +[1] 646-957-9218
www.worldevangelicals.org / wea@worldea.org

While this volume does not represent an "official" position of the World Evangelical Alliance we are distributing it to promote further serious study and reflection.

International Institute for Religious Freedom
of the World Evangelical Alliance
www.iirf.eu / info@iirf.eu

Friedrichstr. 38 2nd Floor 53111 Bonn Germany	PO Box 535 Edgemead 7407 Cape Town South Africa	32, Ebenezer Place Dehiwela (Colombo) Sri Lanka

2nd edition 2017
© Copyright 2013 by
Verlag für Kultur und Wissenschaft
(Culture and Science Publ.)
Prof. Dr. Thomas Schirrmacher
Friedrichstraße 38, 53111 Bonn, Germany
Fax +49 / 228 / 9650389
www.vkwonline.de / info@vkwonline.de

ISBN 978-3-86269-072-5 / ISSN 1867-7320

Printed in Germany
Cover design:
BoD Verlagsservice Beese, Friedensallee 76, 22765 Hamburg, Germany
Production:
CPI Books / Buch Bücher.de GmbH, 96158 Birkach
www.cpi-print.de / info.birkach@cpi-print.de
Publisher's Distribution:
Hänssler Verlag / IC-Medienhaus
71087 Holzgerlingen, Germany, Tel. +49 / 7031/7414-177 Fax -119
www.haenssler.de / www.icmedienhaus.de

Individual sales:
www.mandvbooks.com

The WEA Global Issues Series is sponsored by:
Gebende Hände gGmbH / Giving Hands International
Adenauerallee 11 • 53111 Bonn, Germany • www.giving-hands.de
Martin Bucer Seminary
European Theological School and Research Institutes
Bonn – Zurich – Innsbruck – Prague – Istanbul – São Paulo
www.bucer.org

Contents

Foreword 9
    Ethics for Christians in the World... 9

1. Loving, thinking, working 11
    1.1. Christian leaders are keen to love 12
        God loves 12
        The commandment to love: love as the fulfillment of a value system ... 13
        Boundaries protect love but do not create love.. 15
        Is love pitted against self-love?... 17
        On self-denial 21
    1.2. Christian leaders think and readily love... 21
        God thinks 22
        A Christian is a thinking person... 23
        The reasonable act of worship 25
        Thinking related to reality 28
        Lifelong learning... 28
    1.3. Christian leaders like to work 30
        God is at work: the biblical work ethic is based upon the notion of
        God 30
        The dignity of work.. 32
        Work in the Garden of Eden 33
        The value of work 35
        Authority means work... 36
        The divine and human division of labor 38
        Limiting work: work and rest.. 38
        God as an Employer: without God there is no work.............................. 39
        Work for God 40
        Work for others 42
        The burden of work.. 43
    1.4. The three aspects of every decision 45

2. Normative decisions.. 47
    2.1. Leading normatively means setting values and drawing boundaries 48
        Values and faith... 48
        Are there people who have no ethics? 48
        Sources of vvangelical ethics... 50
        Conclusions from the Bible... 53

2.2. Normative leadership means applying and interpreting 54
   Diverse types of commands 54
   The five levels of law 55
   Case law and ethic of principles 57
   Values are "only" a framework 61
   Helping to translate 67
2.3. Normative leadership means understanding mandates 69
   The four mandates 69
   Different duties according to the four mandates 73
   Different Aspects of the four mandates (by Karl Schock) 74
   The separation of church and state 76
   The mandates belong together 78
   Examples of the dangers of overstepping the boundaries of individual mandates 79

3. Deciding Situationally 82

3.1. Leading situationally means balancing pros and cons and calculating the possible outcome 82
   From normative to situational ethics 82
   Ethical conflict 83
   The example of lying to save life 84
   The example of the Sabbath command 86
   Regarding the justification of deciding in favor of a higher command .. 87
   Deciding without prophecy 92
   In the secular domain 93
   Obligation collisions and compromises 95
   Bigger and smaller sins? 96
   How to react against sin? 97
3.2. To lead situationally means to be wise 98
   Law and wisdom 98
   The 'situational ethics' of wisdom 100
   It doesn't work without advice 101
   The results of our actions 104
   Regarding 'consequentialism' 106

4. Deciding existentially 108

4.1. Leading existentially means internalizing what one does 108
   The internal attitude in the Old Testament 109
4.2. Leading existentially means gaining experience 112
4.3. To existentially lead means to suffer vicariously and to cultivate relationships 114
4.4. To lead existentially means to simultaneously indict and defend 117

4.5. To lead existentially means to be a personality and oneself 120
    God wants an unmistakable personality 120
    The example of God's revelation in his Word via different
    personalities 121
    The meaning of experience for understanding God's revelation 123
4.6. To lead existentially means to decide 'alone' 124

About the Author 127

    Books by Thomas Schirrmacher in chronological order (With short
    commentaries) 127
        As author: 127
        As editor (always with own contributions): 134
    Biography 140

Foreword

Ethics for Christians in the World

In John 17:15-18 Jesus prayed, "My prayer is not that you take them out of the world but that you protect them from the evil one. They are not of the world, even as I am not of it. Sanctify them by the truth; your word is truth. As you sent me into the world, I have sent them into the world."

With these words Jesus clarified a central pattern for the Christian life: *in* the world but not *of* the world. Our identity, purposes, and principles must not come from the world (or cultures) in which we live; we belong, body and soul, to Jesus Christ, who gives us our identity, purposes, and principles. But he does not take us out of the world. Jesus wants us to be *in* the world. Or even more strongly, he has sent us *into* the world. There is continual motion in the Christian life, the motion of people with a global task.

Our world exists in darkness; this is what we see when we read the news, listen to people, or read the Bible. The darkness can seem overwhelming. I am sometimes driven to tears by the events of the day. In response, Jesus said, "I am **the light of the world**. Whoever follows me will never walk in darkness, but will have the light of life." (John 8:12) But Jesus also said to believers, "You are the light of the world." (Matthew 5:14) As those who belong to Jesus Christ, we are sent into the world to bring his light.

It seems to me that the light we have been given to bring into the world is twofold: On the one hand, there is the light which is Jesus himself, the gospel, and the full counsel of God. This light is total and complete. Around the world we see millions of people coming to faith in Jesus and learning to walk in the total truth and light which is Jesus and the Word of God. On the other hand, there is the light of parts of biblical wisdom, which is particular and partial, but nonetheless very important and practical. I am thinking of principles such as, "You must have accurate and honest weights and measures, so that you may live long in the land the LORD your God is giving you" (Deuteronomy 25:15); or observations like, "the lips of the adulterous woman drip honey, and her speech is smoother than oil; but in the end she is bitter as gall, sharp as a double-edged sword. Her feet go down to death; her steps lead straight to the grave." (Proverbs 5:3-5)

Individuals come to faith in Jesus and become lifetime students of the full Word of God. This is the total light which is a process that will continue until eternal life. But partial and particular light is also crucially important, shaping the life of individuals, institutions, and cultures. Such partial light makes more explicit and unfolds the light which God built into creation, which is now often covered by darkness.

Thomas Schirrmacher's delightful book on ethics is written for precisely this dynamic situation: we are learning the whole counsel of God while we are also sent into the world with this two-fold mission. He has devoured the Bible to learn the whole counsel of God and has organized what he learned in light of the some of the best themes from the history of Christian ethics, while always thinking of our twofold mission into the world. His numerous textboxes, whether called "How this can be conveyed to a secular environment" or "An example from the business sector," are not minor additions to the book. The textboxes train us for our second mission, bringing partial and particular light into dark institutions and contexts, the places where many of us work every day. Such partial light has value, whether or not our neighbors come to faith, and this partial light may open doors to talk about the total light of the gospel. Professor Schirrmacher deserves a huge thanks for making such partial light so explicit and practical, while he is also giving us the total view of life which is Christian Ethics.

You will see that Dr. Schirrmacher applies a "Three Aspects" approach to leadership and ethical life: Normative, Situational, and Existential. This is what I would regard as an "industry standard" in evangelical theology in the twenty-first century. It is a development from the way Christians during the Protestant Reformation (in the sixteenth century) described the good works which Christians must practice as following God's law, for God's glory in a fallen world, and motivated by true faith in the gospel. It leads to a very rich and balanced way of understanding of our mission and life before God. I am reminded of the comment of C. S. Lewis, that being a Christian is an education in itself.

So read the truly interesting book by our brother Thomas. Let him prepare you to become a light-bringing leader. This is the calling of Jesus and what our world needs.

Thomas K. Johnson, Ph.D.

1. Loving, thinking, working

Do you think about others only reluctantly? Is it too complicated to love others? Do you not like to reflect about things and prefer to not work? Do you prefer comfortable and simple solutions instead of coming to the best decision for everyone by putting in a lot of effort and contemplation? If so, then you have the wrong book in your hands! In such case you also are not a Christian leader. You surely were not assigned a leadership role by taking an easy path. You would not have become a leader if you do not readily think of others and if deliberation and work do not give you pleasure. Additionally, if you see yourself as a "Christian" leader, it is surely clear to you that you want to – and should – love, think, and work more than others. Jesus did not become our Lord by taking the easy path. Rather, he placed himself in the service of others up to the point of offering himself as a sacrifice.

Before we turn our attention to the question of concrete ways of making decisions, we want to first establish three foundational thoughts. Three things are the conditions for all that follows: 1. the readiness to love, 2. the readiness to think, 3. the readiness to work. In all three cases we want to begin with the idea that God himself loves, thinks, and works. If this is already clear to you, then you can move ahead to the question of decision making in Chapter 2.

A number of passages come under the heading "*How can this be conveyed to a secular environment?*" In the text there are examples and ideas of how Christian convictions can be discussed with people who do not share the basics and the language of the Christian faith. This book seeks to take to heart the necessity of translating normative values into life situations (Chapter 2.2). This means that a dichotomy between a "life of faith" and a "life in the world" should not be established. Radically to the contrary, the practical execution of our faith in everyday life should be fostered. Texts with the heading "*How can this be conveyed to a secular environment?*" refer to the respective passages in which they occur.

In addition, there are passages with the heading "*Example from the Business Sector*" (or *Family, Church, State*), and they include concrete examples from the four spheres of life addressed in Chapter 2.2. Since the main features of ethical decisions are the same in all spheres of life, these examples should help to manage the step from familiar spheres of life to new ground.

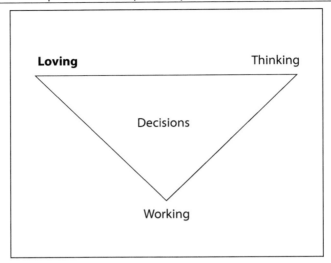

1.1. Christian leaders are keen to love

God loves

Christian ethics[1] is an ethic of love, because "God is love" (1 John 4:8, 16). He is "the God of love" (2 Corinthians 13:11) and Jesus is how "God showed his love among us" (1 John 4:9). For this reason, love has its origination in God's being: "... for love comes from God" (1 John4:7). At the same time God desires. Therefore, to be "in God" and to be "in love" are the same things: "God is love. Whoever lives in love lives in God, and God in him" (1 John 4:16).

The Trinity plays a significant role in anchoring love in the nature of God. At least two individuals are required for love. A counterpart is required. A God who is not Trinitarian can therefore only love when he has created a counterpart. Other monotheistic religions such as post-biblical Judaism or Islam have a more difficult time describing love as an eternal characteristic of God that was present prior to creation. The triune God of the Bible, however, has an eternal love counterpart within himself. Such is the manner in which John 17:24 describes the love of the Father to the Son

---

[1] I have thoroughly addressed many of the questions herein from the perspective of theological ethics in my work entitled *Ethik* (*Ethics,* Second Edition, 3 vols., 2,560 pp., RVB: Hamburg, 2001). Whoever would prefer a more thorough discussion instead of a concentration on practical issues is referred to that work.

1. Loving, thinking, working

before the creation of the world: "Father ... you loved me before the creation of the world."

On account of this, inner-Trinitarian love is the embodiment of love and the starting point of all Christian love and ethics. The persons of the Trinity speak with each other, plan with each other, listen to each other, act for each other, care for each other, honor each other, etc., and that is why all these actions have to do with love and are part of God and part of us as people. If mankind, as the image of God, is able to speak, think plan, act, and care, then all of these characteristics and abilities from the beginning were oriented toward love. Karl Bernhard Hundeshagen, head of Bern University, wrote on this topic in 1853: "The Christian teaching of the Trinity of God is of immeasurable cultural importance, in that it provides the conditions for fully putting humanitarian thought into effect."[2]

How can this be conveyed to a secular environment?
The creation is built upon relationships, and for this reason all values are determined by seeing love as the perfect relationship. It has to do with avoiding harm to others and ourselves and with promoting the good for others and ourselves. This is what is confirmed by oath by the German Chancellor and the Federal Ministers when they take office. There are no values that objectively exist independent of relationships. All values are imbedded in the fact that mankind is unable to completely live alone – one only has to think about the fact that solitary confinement is the worst kind of torment. Jesus' famous Golden Rule makes it clear that we can only live when we live for others and others live for us. "So in everything, do to others what you would have them do to you ..." (Matthew 7:12).

The commandment to love: love as the fulfillment of a value system

Out of the love of God[3] comes the commandment to love. Wilhelm Lütgert writes in his foundational book about love in the New Testament: "With

---

[2] Karl Bernhard Hundeshagen. Ueber die Natur und geschichtliche Entwicklung der Humanitätsidee in ihrem Verhältnis zu Kirche und Staat. Verlag von Wiegen und Grieben: Berlin, 1853. p. 29 (sic); comp. the appraisal of the quote in Theodor Christlieb. "Carl Bernhard Hundeshagen: Eine Lebensskizze." Deutsche Blätter 1873: pp. 673-700, here p. 698.

[3] The three best studies known to me regarding the concept of love in the New Testament are: Wilhelm Lütgert. Die Liebe im Neuen Testament. TVG. Brunnen: Gießen, 1986² (reprint by A. Deichert: Leipzig, 1905¹) – condensed in Wilhelm Lütgert. Schöpfung und Offenbarung. Brunnen: Gießen, 1984² (reprint by Bertelsmann: Gütersloh, 1934¹). pp. 375-398; Leon Morris. Testaments of Love: A Study of Love in the Bible. Wm. B. Eerdmans: Grand Rapids (MI), 1981; Benjamin B. Warfield. "The Terminology of Love in the New Testament." The Princeton Theo-

the commandment to love it is said that love is a duty. It is required and demonstrates obedience. Over against this comes the objection – and Immanuel Kant above all made this objection his own – that one can only command external acts, not love."[4] After all, love is a free act of the will and a deeper, inner, almost subconscious drive. Lütgert does not contradict this, but on his account views love as something that we cannot create on our own. Love presupposes a God of love: "For this reason love can only be commanded by one who can bring it to life. It is first of all something that is given, before it is something that is commanded. It is a gift before it is a task. It emerges out of love and is always requited love. Therefore it can only be a gift of the Creator, an echo of his love, which as a love of the Creator is itself creative. Augustine's rule[5] applies to love: Command what You will, and then grant what you command."[6]

Due to this, the dual Old Testament commandment of love, to love God and one's neighbor, is always in the center of Old Testament law. Martin Luther repeatedly made this clear in his Small Catechism, which included an interpretation of the Ten Commandments.[7] We are not dealing with two separate commandments, but actually the same thing.[8]

Accordingly, the commandment to love is not just any commandment. Rather, each commandment and each decision acquires its importance in love and is oriented towards love.[9] Paul therefore writes the following: "The goal of this command is love, which comes from a pure heart and a good conscience and a sincere faith" (1 Timothy 1:5). At another point he says: "Let no debt remain outstanding, except the continuing debt to love one another, for he who loves his fellowman has fulfilled the law. The commandments, "Do not commit adultery," "Do not murder," "Do not steal," "Do not covet," and whatever other commandment there may be, are summed up in this one rule: "Love your neighbor as yourself." Love

---

logical Review 16 (1918): pp. 1-45, 153-203, in Benjamin B. Warfield. *Biblical Doctrines*. The Banner of Truth Trust: Edinburgh, 1988 (reprint from 1929). pp. 511-597.

[4] Wilhelm Lütgert. Ethik der Liebe. Beiträge zur Förderung christlicher Theologie. Series 2, vol. 29. C. Bertelsmann: Gütersloh, 1938. p. 30.

[5] Augustine directs the following appeal to God.

[6] Ibid.

[7] Ulrich Asendorf. Die Theologie Martin Luthers nach seinen Predigten. Vandenhoeck & Ruprecht: Göttingen, 1988. pp. 305-314+406-417 has shown that this is expressed in innumerable sermons by Martin Luther.

[8] John thoroughly substantiates this in throughout 1 John (esp. 1 John 4:4-5:3).

[9] Comp. above all Wilhelm Lütgert. Die Liebe im Neuen Testament. op.cit. pp. 82-85.

does no harm to its neighbor. Therefore love is the fulfillment of the law" (Romans 13:8-10). Whoever has truly practiced love will "automatically" fulfill the law. Paul quotes as an example four of the Ten Commandments (Romans 13:9), and the tenth he presents in abridged form ("You shall not covet").

Paul immediately adds the following to the examples from the Ten Commandments: "... and whatever other commandment there may be ..." (Romans 13:9), such that he principally means all commandments and regulations. All commandments are, then, summarized in the statement "Love your neighbor as yourself" (Romans 13:9). This statement itself comes from the Old Testament law (Leviticus 19:18). The idea that love is the fulfillment of the law is not something that is added in the New Testament. Rather, it is determinate of the nature of the Old Testament law itself. The Ten Commandments are only implementation statutes of the commandment to love. This is on account of the fact that whoever loves God will only honor him, and whoever loves his neighbor will not kill him, steal from him, or lie to him.

James uses the same Old Testament quotation to summarize the meaning of all the commandments and to explicate the Ten Commandments from the standpoint of love. After he speaks in James 2:1-8 about practical examples of discriminating against poor Christians in the local church, he states: "If you really keep the royal law found in Scripture, 'Love your neighbor as yourself,' you are doing right. But if you show favoritism, you sin and are convicted by the law as lawbreakers. For whoever keeps the whole law and yet stumbles at just one point is guilty of breaking all of it. For he who said, 'You shall not commit adultery,' also said, 'You shall not murder.' If you do not commit adultery but do commit murder, you have become a lawbreaker. Speak and act as those who are going to be judged by the law that gives freedom" (James 2:8-12).

Whoever has gone over a wall at one point is over the entire wall. And this wall of the law is the commandment of love that one can climb over at many points. The expression "the royal law" means the law that rules over or has dominion over all other law. Because the law is determined by love, the commandment to love is "the royal law" and "the law that gives freedom," whereby that last notion simultaneously characterizes the entire word of God.

Boundaries protect love but do not create love

On account of the above, the commandments of God and the basic values of the creation can never come into conflict with love. Only if boundaries are trespassed is love endangered. Paul writes in this connection: "But the fruit of the Spirit is love, joy, peace, patience, kindness, goodness, faithfulness, gentleness and self-control. Against such things there is no law" (Galatians 5:22-23).

As correct as the law is, one must resist the misunderstanding that the law alone can create love. The commandment, for example, protects marriage against adultery, hatred, etc. True marital love will also fulfill the law towards one's partner. And still, marital love encompasses significantly more. What partners in marriage do for each other, and are for each other, cannot simply be derived from commandments. Rather, these things correspond to the personal relationship between two people, and that differentiates them from all other people. The law is like a house that has to be very carefully built. Love, by contrast, corresponds to the dwellers who give the house its sense. Whoever only concerns himself with the law is like an architect who builds a house for its own sake and forgets that a house is there to serve people as a home and place of protection. In the book of Job one can read the following: "I have not departed from the commands of his lips; I have treasured the words of his mouth more than my daily bread" (Job 23:12). Job's love for the poor, which is being described in this connection, went far beyond the requirements of the law.

Nevertheless, from this fact one should never come to the opposite conclusion, which is that love could do without values and the law. If love goes beyond the requirement of the law, in such case it is never acting against the commandment but sees in the law love's framework and duty.

How can this be conveyed to a Secular Environment?
What the consequences are when talking about love, without listing any rules of implementation, can be illustrated by numerous examples from daily life. How, for instance, could a soccer match proceed if its only rule were "fairness"?[10] Fairness in sports is a good thing, but without rules that implement it, fairness is senseless and ineffective. Every soccer player would understand "fairness" as something else.

Example from the business sector

Laws against sexual harassment in the workplace are important. It is also important for a company to create the necessary structures for its female employees so that action can be taken against harassment. In order to implement boundaries, it is not necessary that an offender share the attitude of the state or of the company. However, it is desirable that men act out of

---

[10] This example comes from Erwin Lutzer. Measuring Morality: A Comparison of Ethical Systems. Probe Ministries Int.: Dallas (TX), 1989. p. 36.

internal conviction and out of respect for women. On account of this, a wise company will not only set boundaries and structures of prevention. It will also look for ways to mentally win over as many employees as possible. That could come by offering literature and training. It could also come by offering opportunities to discuss issues either in discussion groups, in which women could present their impressions and what they would appreciate, or by making concrete offers of therapy to potential offenders with a trained co-worker or with someone from outside the company.

Is love pitted against self-love?

By connecting love with the commandments of God, the question of love for oneself in the statement "love your neighbor as yourself" is also clarified. Some people understand this statement as a general call that one first has to love oneself before one can love others. Others see every sort of love for oneself as the end of the self-denial called for by Jesus (Matthew 16:24; Mark 8:34; Luke 9:23) and understand "as yourself" as a concession regarding the unfortunately ever-present egoism.[11] If one takes the commandments of God, one can see that both sides are correct and incorrect in equal measure. *If God has commanded us to care for ourselves and to create our own joy, then at this point no basic self-denial can be called for.* If God has assigned us the task of earning our living or to delight in food, then such a commitment to ourselves cannot be wrong. *Where God however assigns us the task of placing the interests of others above our own, we trample such values under foot at our own peril.* Wilhelm Lütgert has stated this strikingly: "If through love to God selfishness is eliminated from self preservation, it then becomes love of self... . Selfishness is not love of self. The selfish person does not love at all, not even himself."[12]

The Bible does not pit the individual and society, nor individual interests and others' interests, against each other. It is neither purely individualistic nor purely socialistic. The Bible safeguards the individual's private sphere

---

[11] Regarding the history of the concept of egoism since Immanuel Kant employed this concept in ethics, comp. Heinz-Horst Schrey. "Egoismus." pp. 304-308 in: Gerhard Müller (ed.). Theologische Realenzyklopädie. vol. 9. de Gruyter: Berlin, 1993/1982 (Study Edition). Therein, on p. 306 it is aptly stated "Daß der Egoismus als Ichzentriertheit des Menschen ein Merkmal der Moderne ist, kann als allgemein anerkanntes Axiom der neueren Kultursoziologie und -psychologie gelten." ("Egoism as a centering on the self is an identifier of modern times and can be seen as a generally recognized axiom of newer cultural sociology and cultural psychology.")

[12] Wilhelm Lütgert. Ethik der Liebe. op. cit., p. 17.

(Proverbs 25:16-17) and by the same token exempts no one from social responsibility.

Jesus' famous golden rule inseparably joins love for oneself and a life lived for others with each other: "So in everything, do to others what you would have them do to you, for this sums up the Law and the Prophets" (Matthew 7:12). For this reason one can only agree the economist George Gilder who says: "The belief that the happiness of others in the end also helps oneself finds its way with difficulty to the human heart. Nevertheless, this is the golden rule of the economy, the key to peace and prosperity, and a precondition for progress."[13]

In two respects the Bible establishes the reasons for the highest goal of man, namely to achieve eternal life and to live in eternal fellowship with God. On the one hand, God receives the primary position, and mankind is to submit humbly to God's will: Mankind will inevitably glorify God eternally as his Lord and Savior. On the other hand, this is actually the best thing that a person could do for himself. On account of this the Bible, without limitation, substantiates a life according to the will of God with the benefit that man will receive from it in eternity (e.g., Ephesians 6:8; Colossians 3:23-24; John 4:36; comp. 1 Timothy 6:19). Eternal fellowship with God is the consummation of love toward God, of love toward others, and of true love of one's own life. It is therefore the consummation of the desire to make the best out of one's own life.

Example from family life

> Marriage is the best example of the way love of oneself and love for others belong together. The marriage partner indeed promises to live completely for the other person and in the extreme case to put his or her life on the line for the other. But this only works because the other partner also promises the same. Whoever marries invests fully in another person and is at the same time the greatest beneficiary. Paul writes therefore without any hint of a bad conscience: "He who loves his wife loves himself" (Ephesians 5:28b). This thinking is behind Paul's logic when he says the following about loving one's wife: "After all, no one ever hated his own body" (Ephesians 5:29a). According to Paul, fulfilled sexuality means, therefore. that each gives priority to the other: "The husband should fulfill his marital duty to his wife, and likewise the wife to her husband. The wife's body does not belong to her alone but also to her husband. In the same way, the husband's body does not belong to him alone but also to his wife. Do not deprive each other except by mutual consent and for a time …" (1 Corinthians 7:3-5a). This sexual equality is completely based on reciprocity and not only breaks down if both are

---

[13] George Gilder. Reichtum und Armut. dtv: München, 1983. p. 19.

egoists. Rather, it also breaks down if only one partner ceases to support the other.

Example from the business sector

Work is another good example of the two-sided orientation of love, as we will later see. Work is simultaneously both for the benefit of the one working (e.g., by earning a livelihood as a shoemaker) and working for others (e.g., by repairing shoes). In the case of the wealthy, the enjoyment of wealth and the use of wealth for others are not mutually exclusive: "Command those who are rich in this present world not to be arrogant nor to put their hope in wealth, which is so uncertain, but to put their hope in God, who richly provides us with everything for our enjoyment. Command them to do good, to be rich in good deeds, and to be generous and willing to share. In this way they will lay up treasure for themselves as a firm foundation for the coming age, so that they may take hold of the life that is truly life" (1 Timothy 6:17-19). Wealth should serve one's own enjoyment as well as serve others, whereby the latter will benefit the giver in heaven.

Example from the political sector

The modern theory of the state is in accord with the Bible and was, at this point, influenced by it. This idea is that the state is based on an agreement between the governed and the governing. The state is there for its citizens, and the citizen is there for the state. Only if both are mutually there for each other can the state function. If those who govern live too much for themselves and too little for the people, a dictatorship arises. A dictatorship can last for a very long time, but in the end it will fall apart. If too many of the governed only live for themselves and do a disservice to the state and the common good, the state also breaks down. For example, this can occur if the state does not receive adequate finances via taxes or if so many people are incarcerated that the remaining citizens can no longer carry the burden.

How can this be conveyed to a secular environment?

Example from the political sector

Many problems arise where things are pitted against each other that God in his revelation has related to each other. This applies to individualism and collectivism. Individualism sees the individual, each individual person, as the most important measure. Individualism believes that everything has to align itself to the needs and desires of the individual. This is, for instance, the message of political liberalism. Collectivism, in contrast, views the community (of the church, state, etc.) as the most important measure. Collectivism believes that all private needs are to be subordinated to the welfare of the community. This becomes particularly clear in communism, for instance, or in the slogan of national socialism: "You are nothing, the nation is everything." This one-sidedness still casts humanity into large difficulties. Only a balance between advocating the individual and an orientation towards the interests of the community can bring about a humane coexistence in the family as well as in the church, in the economy as well as in the state.

In the Bible the juxtaposition of individualism and collectivism is overcome by the fact that neither the individual nor the community is the measure and end of human life. Rather, it is God and his glory. God is the one who in his word ascribes to the individual and to the community equal importance. However, the importance is not only of community but of community in various associations, for instance in living and working together in family, church, the economy, and the state. The protection of the individual, as much as the protection of the community, is considered equally and regulated by God's commandments. Only on the basis of God's commandments can we experience in which cases which area receives the "right of way."

Francis Schaeffer made it clear that overcoming the tension between the one and the many is a central and unresolved problem in the history of philosophy, which in the Bible is conclusively resolved in the Trinity of God: "There are two problems which always exist – the need for unity and the need for diversity."[14] Every philosophy has this problem and no philosophy has an answer. "But with the doctrine of the Trinity, the unity and diversity is God Himself – three Persons, yet one God. That is what the Trinity is, and nothing less than this. We muss appreciate that our Christian forefathers understood this very well in A.D. 325, when they stressed the three Persons in the Trinity, as the Bible had clearly set this forth. Let us notice that it is not that they invented the Trinity in order to give an answer to the philosophical questions which the Greeks of that time understood. It is quite the contrary. The Unity and diversity problem was there, and the Christians realized that in the Trinity, as it had been taught in the Bible, they had an answer that no one else had. They did not invent the Trinity to meet the need; the Trinity was already there and it met the need. They realized that in the Trinity we have what all these people are arguing about and defining but for which they have no answer."[15]

---

[14] Francis Schaeffer. He is there and He is not silent. in: The Complete Works of Francis Schaeffer. Vol. 1. Wheaton (IL): Crossways, 1991-2. p. 284.

[15] Ibid., p. 289.

On self-denial

I would like to say another word about self-denial. When Jesus makes a call for self-denial and requests that one take up one's cross, he is not speaking about a psychological term – for instance self contempt or insufficient self-confidence. Rather, he is simply calling for preparedness for martyrdom, a preparedness to die for the faith:[16] "Then Jesus said to his disciples, 'If anyone would come after me, he must deny himself and take up his cross and follow me. For whoever wants to save his life will lose it, but whoever loses his life for me will find it'" (Matthew 16-24-25). This passage comes out of the first long talk on martyrdom that Jesus gives in Matthew 10:16-42. Self-denial means placing God principally and without exception in the first position and, on account of that, being ready to experience martyrdom. Self-denial in no wise means placing every other person in the first position or to deny oneself every pleasure. It is through submission to God that one comes to understand the correct way to interact with other people and with the goods which God gives us.

1.2. Christian leaders think and readily love

"Have you ever visited one of those East European countries where members of the militia always walk around in groups of three? One says that it is for the following reason: the first one can read, the second one is skillful in writing, and the third one has the task of keeping an eye on the two intellectuals. Nowadays there is a similar situation in many churches. Whoever can speak intelligently for more than two minutes and thereby mentions more than one thought per minute is seen as a dangerous, unspiritual intellectual. Nevertheless, today's church faces large problems and difficulties, and they need to be thoroughly thought through in light of God's word and in light of the current world situation. We have to refrain from giving simple answers to difficult questions. We have to demonstrate a willingness to pray, to reflect, and to conduct the hard intellectual labor so that we can determine what our present position is and what the Lord desires of us."[17]

---

[16] For a more lengthy discussion see Thomas Schirrmacher. The Persecution of Christians Concerns Us All. Bonn: VKW, 2009, 2nd. ed.

[17] Francis Schaeffer's associate Os Guinness addresses the question of how western Christianity can survive in: Os Guinness. Des Teufels Fehde-Handschuh: Kirche und Gesellschaft. Verlag der Francke-Buchhandlung. Marburg, 1991. p. 3.

God thinks

God thinks and man thinks because man is made in the image of God. The Bible often speaks about thinking and the thoughts of God. Twenty-six times in the Old Testament the Bible speaks of the "heart" of God[18] or about the fact that God "speaks in his heart." God says with regard to a new priest in 1 Samuel 2:35: "I will raise up for myself a faithful priest, who will do according to what is in my heart and mind." It is to be noted that in Hebrew parallelism the words "heart" and "mind" are equated with each other. In Psalm 33:10-11, "the purposes of his heart," referring to God's thoughts, is contrasted with "the plans of the nations," or thoughts of people. In Jeremiah 44:21 one reads: "Did not the Lord remember and think about the incense burned in the towns of Judah and the streets of Jerusalem by you and your fathers, your kings and your officials and the people of the land?" (RSV).

Mankind thinks as an image of God (Genesis 1:26-27), because it is God "who forms the hearts of all" (Psalm 33:15a). The first manifestations of life of which the Bible reports in the creation account are for this reason connected with thinking, be it conversation with God or the serpent, or be it the task of naming all the animals (Genesis 2: 19-20).

The heart is the center of a person. It is quite simply the decision-making center of a person. The heart, then, mirrors the image of God like scarcely anything else and for that reason is indispensible for God's communication with mankind and for mankind's communication with each other.

In our heart and in our thinking we can see the true character of our relationship with God. One of the most important verses in the Old and New Testaments makes this clear: "Love the Lord your God with all your heart and with all your soul and with all your strength and with all your mind" (Luke 10:27).[19] This verse does not give us a list of delimited parts in a person. Rather, it presents overlapping designations for the crucial center of the individual.

On account of the central importance the Bible places on the heart and, with that, thinking and planning, nothing has to be paid more attention to than one's own heart: "Above all else, guard your heart, for it is the wellspring of life" (Proverbs 4:23). What we think and decide determines our life.

---

[18] Hans Walter Wolff. Anthropologie des Alten Testaments. Chr. Kaiser: München, 1977³. p. 68.

[19] Similarly Mark 12:30; quoted from Deuteronomy 6.5, Israel's focal confession of faith; similarly Deuteronomy 10:12; 11:13; Joshua 22:5.

A Christian is a thinking person

According to the Bible, a Christian is for this reason a thinking person, and indeed someone who consciously and readily thinks.[20] Paul therefore summons Christians as follows: "Brothers and sisters, stop thinking like children. In regard to evil be infants, but in your thinking be adults" (1 Corinthians 14:20).

Herbert Schlossberg and Marvin Olasky have made it very clear that Christian thinking is threatened from two sides.[21] On the one side there is rationalism, which raises reason to the position of highest authority and thereby misuses this gift of God, reason.[22] On the other side is quietism,[23] which holds thinking to be principally bad and places faith more in the category of our feelings where it is attached to private piety. For these authors, the world has been broken down into two categories. There is a private, religious, feeling-based side that has to do with faith that cannot be reasonably discussed. And there is a secular, purely reason-based side of knowledge that can be discussed. This breakdown traces back, above all, to Immanuel Kant.[24] Ultimately it dates back to attempts to preserve for religious people an untouchable inner sanctuary of feelings against the growing pressure of rationalism. Such attempts fail, because the religious individual continually has to pull back and sacrifice additional parts of life and the entire creation. Lastly, psychology also made inner religious life an area of debate. In the Bible, on the other hand, we are dealing with precisely the opposite, which is to submit all thinking, to make it obedient to Christ (2 Corinthians 10:3-6).

---

[20] Manfried Schulte offers a good overview. "Verstand." Das Fundament (DCTB) 84 (1987) 6: pp. 28-30; "The Law of a Sound Mind." Sword and Trowel 2/1987: pp. 24-27; John R. W. Stott. Es kommt auch auf den Verstand an. Telos. Hänssler: Neuhausen, 1975. It would not be possible to list all the concepts and texts in the New Testament where thinking is indispensible for carrying out a life of faith. Christians 'know,' 'realize,' 'learn,' and 'teach,' 'ask' and 'answer,' ask for 'wisdom' and 'intelligence,' 'understand' and 'comprehend,' 'test,' 'explain,' etc. Compare "New Testament Words About the Use of the Believer's Mind." Sword and Trowel 2/1987: pp. 27-30.

[21] Herbert Schlossberg, Marvin Olasky. Turning Point: A Christian Worldview Declaration. Crossway Books: Westchester (IL), 1987.

[22] Ibid., part. pp. 61-70.

[23] Actually 'pietism,' although in American English 'pietism' often has a different meaning than in German.

[24] Ibid., particularly pp. 36-37.

Example from family life

In the Bible both the act of marriage and the state of being married, including the sexual relationship, are described as "knowing" the marriage partner (Genesis 4:1,17,25; 19:8; 24:16; 1 Kings 1:4; Matthew 1:25).[25] For instance, this is the case where it is stated that "Adam knew his wife Eve" (Genesis 4:1) and that thereafter a son was born. Knowing includes intellectual recognition and getting to know someone as well as desire and a complete relationship. On account of this, marriage does not only include living together and expressing sexuality. Rather, it includes continual conversation, counsel, intensive exchanges, and thinking oneself into the position of the other. A marriage in which understanding of the other dies out and the thought of the other person no longer is of interest is a dying marriage.

A God-fearing person in the Old Testament is a person who contemplates and does not live thoughtlessly for the moment. This is repeatedly emphasized in the Proverbs, for instance when Proverbs refers to speaking: "The heart of the righteous weighs its answers, but the mouth of the wicked gushes evil" (Proverbs 15:28). "A simple man believes anything, but a prudent man gives thought to his steps" (Proverbs 14:15). Christians know what they do, and they do not live blindly for the moment.

"Self-control,"[26] which is so often referenced in the New Testament, has much to do with not following our impulse. Rather, it has to do with thinking and then acting (Acts 24:25; 2 Peter 1:6; 1 Corinthians 7:29; 9:25; Titus 1:8). What is more often recommended is deliberateness, that is, to think things through calmly. It is always identified as a characteristic which should distinguish Christians (e.g., Romans 12:3; 1 Peter 4:7; comp. Proverbs 1:4).

Example from church life

This sober-mindedness is seen above all as a precondition for taking on a position of leadership in the church (2 Timothy 1:7; Titus 2:6, 12). Why? Because leadership is always tied to taking time and deliberating, consulting with others, and deciding only after careful consideration. An elder or a pastor does not immediately react fiercely to rumors. Rather, he takes his time to speak with all involved parties, to consult with others, and then to support the most sensible way towards a process of conflict resolution. For example, in the case of excommunication from the church, the New Testament re-

---

[25] Comp. ibid., p. 113.

[26] The Greek is 'enkrateia,' with other meanings: self-control, abstinence, chastity, temperance, sober-mindedness. The opposite is a lack of self control, lack of discipline, lawlessness, immoderateness.

quires several levels of discussion in order to ensure that no premature decision is made. Also, in the case of difficult questions and problems, an elder does not hit the panic button. On the contrary, he seeks the best solution in a calm and sober manner.

Example from family life

For children in Christian families there can be a big problem where parents lead a pious life but do not know *why* they do things in one way or another. The role model the parents play is enormously important, but if parents have not thought about why they think something is important or foundationally wrong, the children have no opportunity to determine their own point of view. Either they can copy everything they experience, or they can throw it all overboard. The goal, however, is that the children understand why parents act the way they do, in order to later be in a position, in completely different situations, to apply the same wisdom. It can be stated another way: only when parents themselves think about their own lives can they pass on this wisdom to their children. When Peter calls for the following: "Always be prepared to give an answer to everyone who asks you to give the reason for the hope that you have" (1 Peter 3:15), this applies to everyone, including one's own children. A person can only give an account in front of others if he has given account to himself of the same. Only then can children be in a position of later being able to distinguish what was incidental but not of lasting value for their lives (e.g., that shoes belong in the shoe cabinet, or that the Bible is read at 6 a.m. each day), and what was an expression of a basic value and of importance for adult life (e.g., being friendly towards foreigners, giving financial aid to needy people).

The reasonable act of worship

Paul makes a very close connection between a Christian's orientation toward God that includes all areas of life and the desired thinking of a Christian when he writes: "Therefore, I urge you, brothers, in view of God's mercy, to offer your bodies as living sacrifices, holy and pleasing to God – this is your spiritual act of worship. Do not conform any longer to the pattern of this world, but be transformed by the renewing of your mind. Then you will be able to test and approve what God's will is – his good, pleasing and perfect will" (Romans 12:1-2).

Worship is only a "reasonable act of worship" (Romans 12:1) when we not only serve God on Sundays for one to two hours, but rather when we serve him throughout the entire week and in all areas of life. The entire importance of the "reasonable" act of worship does not become clear until one thinks about the fact that Paul, in using the word related to "reasonable" in Romans 1:20 (to "understand" God's invisible qualities), designates the act of worship that man refuses to conduct and thereby becomes a fool. Whoever serves God – as is described in Romans 12:1-2 – finally becomes "reasonable" again in that he or she once again serves the Creator and not the creation (idols, mammon, oneself), the latter being what constitutes an unreasonable act of worship.

It is no wonder that in Romans 12:2 thinking (Greek *nous*, "reason"; often translated with "mind") plays such a role in faith. The central words "conversion," "reversal," or "repentance" (Greek *metanoia*) are derived from the Greek word *nous* and mean so much as "to receive another mind" or to "change one's thinking." To become a Christian means to "change one's thinking." Given this set of circumstances, how can one maintain that faith means dispensing with thinking?

A change in our everyday life begins in our hearts. Only when our thinking is submitted to God's will are we able to have all areas of life embraced by "renewal." Reason, that according to Romans 1:18-32 has to be surrendered in order to not serve God, can again receive what it was originally intended to have: a state in which we can comprehend God's revealed will and serve him. By God's grace, reason receives an unforeseen dignity. How could Christians ever come upon the idea that reason is purportedly a problem, even something that is in the best case completely avoided. How are we to study God's word without reason? The Scriptures state, "The fear of the LORD is the beginning of knowledge" (Proverbs 1:7), not the 'end' of knowledge![27] "Do not conform any longer to the pattern of this world" (Romans 12:2) means as much as to "not follow the schema of this world."[28] One could freely translate the words as follows: "Do not adapt to the Zeitgeist (spirit of the age)." Christians are not 'adapters,' nor are they 'grovelers' who jump on the next bandwagon. Rather, Christians are to consciously reflect about things whereas others only go with the flow.

Paul contrasts the "world" (or the "age") and the "will of God" at this point. It becomes evident from this that what is meant with the word "world" is not the creation or all people. Rather, "world" is an ethical or moral term and means everything that sets itself up against God and his

---

[27] Comp. John R. W. Stott. Es kommt auch auf den Verstand an. op.cit. (all). Johannes Calvin. Unterricht in der christlichen Religion: Institutio Religionis Christianae. Neukirchener Verlag: Neukirchen, 1988^5. p. 151-156 (Book II, Chapter 2, Section 12-19) as well as Manfried Schulte's excellent thesis, "Verstand." Fundament (DCTB) 84 (1987) 6: 28-30.

[28] Greek 'syschematidso,' from 'syn' = 'with' and 'schema' = attitude, nature, pattern, from which we have 'scheme.' Comp. Friedrich Godet. Kommentar zu dem Brief an die Römer. Part 2. Carl Meyer: Hannover, 1893. pp. 244-245.

1. Loving, thinking, working

will and denies his values.[29] This is similarly and clearly expressed in 1 John 2:17: "The world and its desires pass away, but the man who does the will of God lives forever" (1John 2:17). It therefore has to do with practicing God's will. Spiritually 'mature' people are those "who by constant use have trained themselves to distinguish good from evil" (Hebrews 5:14b).

Certainly Christians plan and think subject to God's sovereign rule over the world. For this reason we should not boast about our plans, as if we determine the history of the world (James 4:13-17). Instead, we ought to say, "If it is the Lord's will, we will live and do this or that" (James 4:15). This does not mean, however, that we are not to think rigorously and should not plan. Completely to the contrary, we should – with reasonable reservation – still plan for the future, do our work, and say, "… we will … do this or that" (James 4:15b).

For this reason it must be emphasized that all these terms in the Bible do not mean intellectual ability alone. Rather, they point to an integrated approach, which admittedly is to be understood under intellectual guidance.[30] And what we first said about love should not now be lost.

How can this be conveyed to a secular environment?
Mankind is differentiated from animals by the fact that he thinks and plans, as well as by his being in a position to take responsibility for his actions. The dignity given by God to man does not depend on man's ability to think; otherwise, the unborn, mentally handicapped, and those suffering dementia would not be humans. The dignity of man is a value in itself and is not tied to performance. However, it is this inviolable dignity that, under normal circumstances, leads to man's ability to deliberate and decide and to discuss and share such decisions with others. On account of this, human rights protect man's dignity by protecting man's thinking, especially his conscience and his faith. Love is reliant upon thought and communication. Whoever wants to put love into practice has to be prepared to invest a lot of time in order to address the issues of thought, conscience, and counsel along the path to making a decision that has the greatest benefit for everyone involved and that can be justified.

---

[29] Comp. Kurt Hennig (ed.). Jerusalemer Bibellexikon. Hänssler: Neuhausen, 1989. pp. 931-932; Gary DeMar. 'You Have Heard it Said:' 15 Biblical Misconceptions that Render Christians Powerless. Wolgemuth & Hyatt: Brentwood (TN), 1991. pp. 16-21.

[30] Also Friso Melzer. Das Wort in den Wörtern: Die deutsche Sprache im Lichte der Christus-Nachfolge: Ein theo-philologisches Wörterbuch. J. C. B. Mohr: Tübingen, 1965. pp. 112-113.

Thinking related to reality

We want to briefly address one misunderstanding at this point when we speak about thinking, and that is in connection with the Bible. Whether one has mulled over things is not evidenced by certain academic symbols and rituals (e.g., lengthy footnotes, difficult to understand insider vocabulary and jargon, and titles). Rather, it is shown by what really is. "Thinking" in this context does not mean presenting some theoretical insights in an impressive manner, but rather the deliberate and purposeful planning of our everyday decisions. Regarding this point Rolf Hille writes: "Hence it is not a strength but rather a weakness of academic theology in the Western tradition that an ideal of theoretical knowledge is sought in philosophical and traditional theological concepts. Biblical truth is very practical, and all theological research has to demonstrate spiritual relevance for the practice of church life."[31]

We will still address the idea that it is in fact the task of the church to help Christians 'translate' the Bible into concrete areas of their lives.

Lifelong learning

It can be seen in the Old Testament that the term learner (student), which in our Bible translations is most often expressed with the word disciple, is a standing designation for people who have faith in God (e.g., Isaiah 50:4-5). In German the word for disciple is **Jünger** and is derived from 'jung' (meaning 'young'). It was used as a calque for the Latin junior, meaning learner, apprentice, subordinate[32] and corresponding to the Latin discipulus[33] (comp. English 'disciple') for learner. Above all it is used to translate the Greek word mathetes, which is first used to designate the twelve Apostles as Jesus' disciples (always in John and initially found in John 2:2) and later, however, to designate all followers of Jesus (e.g., Luke 6:17; expressly in Acts 9:25). The standard term for a Christian is therefore learner (student). The Great Commission assumes this designation and explicitly mentions the teaching and doing of the one who has learned: "Therefore go and

---

[31] Rolf Hille. "Der Umbruch von Kirche und Gesellschaft – auf dem Weg zu einer evangelikalen Theologie." pp. 135-152 in: Werner Beyer. Einheit in der Vielfalt: Aus 150 Jahren Evangelischer Allianz. R. Brockhaus: Wuppertal, 1995. p. 146.

[32] Friso Melzer. Das Wort in den Wörtern: Die deutsche Sprache im Lichte der Christus-Nachfolge: Ein theo-philologisches Wörterbuch. J. C. B. Mohr: Tübingen, 1965. p. 237.

[33] Comp. idid. pp. 237-238.

make disciples[34] [or make learners (students)] of all nations ... and teaching them to obey everything I have commanded you" (Matthew 18-20a).

Christians are students who learn their entire lives. It is the specific feature of wisdom to not stop learning, but rather to always continue to learn more. Whoever knows much also knows how much he still does not know. And whoever has learned a lot also knows that he must still learn much: "Do not rebuke a mocker or he will hate you; rebuke a wise man and he will love you. Instruct a wise man and he will be wiser still; teach a righteous man and he will add to his learning. The fear of the Lord is the beginning of wisdom, and knowledge of the Holy One [God] is understanding" (Proverbs 9:8-10).

The book of Proverbs is the Bible's great education book. In the Bible a holistic upbringing encompasses the ability to endure everyday life and to be able to live with other people (for instance in work, caring for others, bringing about peace, achieving justice), and it ties everything to the starting point: "The fear of the LORD is the beginning of wisdom" (Proverbs 9:10; similarly 1:7; comp. Job 28:28; Proverbs 15:33; Psalm 111:10).

Example from family life

In the book of Proverbs it is the declared goal that *learners* learn "wisdom" – the precondition for independence – by following the educator's and God's commands. Wisdom comprises not only an intellectual ability but also the ability to put good knowledge into practice and to use it correctly when living with others (e.g., Proverbs 4:1-9). Parents should therefore not only teach their children what they have learned themselves; rather, they should also teach 1) how and why they learned what they learned, 2) how one can use what has been learned in a new way, 3) how one learns so that throughout life, by applying what has been learned and in new learning, one can wisely respond to new situations.

Example from church life

The task of Christ's church is also not one of making its members learn things once and for all by rote. The task is to teach members from the Bible and from life. Even in theological studies one can only teach a fraction of that which one needs for life in general or as a leader in the church. On account of this, formal theological study should above all teach *how to learn*

---

[34] In the German original I use a single word, the verb *jüngern* instead of the theologically misunderstandable 'make disciples of.' This makes it clear that in the Greek the word for 'make' is not used and that disciples are not 'made' but rather trained. (In German the use of the umlaut and the suffix *–ern* produces a word that expresses 'to make,' e.g., to make pregnant = *schwängern*; lengthen = *verlängern*.)

and not only *material to learn*. The result is that throughout his entire life the graduate should be able to deal with new situations by utilizing the Bible and the experience of being continually open to new things.[35]

Siegfried Buchholz has made it clear that the question of lifelong learning is also one of the greatest challenges for Christians in business: "Trait No. 2 is the way we address education and training. We have to assume that education will be the most important resource of this century. Our present educational system does not prepare its students for the future. The educational system cannot or does not want to understand what is actually necessary for career life. School is still in the business of the pure transmission of knowledge that is traditionally transmissible and can be stored. The educational system still assumes that it is preparing its students for traditional, lifelong careers that in fact no longer exist. The educational system has to learn to prepare students for employability, not employment, i.e., the readiness and ability to jump on the moving train of continually changing careers. That is something that is not learned in school. A global race already began some time ago to see who the best performers will be."[36]

1.3. Christian leaders like to work

God is at work: the biblical work ethic is based upon the notion of God

Affluence and wealth are not only a question of possessions measured in the form of money or other forms of value. In this sense Saudi Arabia would be immensely wealthy. But as far as what relates to issues of manpower, the wealth of ideas of the individual, productivity, innovation and prospects for the future beyond the era of flowing oil, Saudi Arabia remains a poor country.[37] George Gilder looks to a similar example from

---

[35] Comp. my article "Ausbilden wie Jesus und Paulus." pp. 7-43 in: Klaus W. Müller, Thomas Schirrmacher (ed.). Ausbildung als missionarischer Auftrag. Referate der Jahrestagung 1999 in the aforementioned edition – mission reports 7. Verlag für Kultur und Wissenschaft: Bonn, 1999; "Having a Role Model, Being a Role Model." Training for Crosscultural Ministries (World Evangelical Fellowship) 1/2001: 4-7; "Jesus as Master Educator and Trainer." Training for Crosscultural Ministries (World Evangelical Fellowship) 2/2000: 1-4; "Paul and His Colleagues". Training for Crosscultural Ministries (World Evangelical Fellowship) 3/2000: 6-8.

[36] Siegfried Buchholz. "Fit für die Zukunft – Aufspringen auf einen fahrenden Zug." pp. 7-20 in: Jörg Knoblauch, Horst Marquart (ed.). Fit für die Zukunft: Konzepte christlicher Führungskräfte. Brunnen: Gießen, 1999. pp. 13-14.

[37] Cf. George Gilder. Reichtum und Armut. dtv: München, 1983. pp. 64-65.

1. Loving, thinking, working

history: "Four hundred years ago Spain was as rich as Saudi Arabia is today. Silver from the Bolivian Potosi mines bestowed upon the country a vast flood of money. Spain, however, was not able to convert it into true affluence, such that the country soon fell back into its earlier poverty. This happened while what looked like the poorer countries in Europe flourished with industry."[38]

A significant factor in prosperity is work and the profit realized from the work that is done. On account of this, every set of business ethics and every actual condition of the economy has to do with the *work ethic*, a notion which indicates *that there is no work without morality, and that work is always the effluence of an ethical point of view.*

The Christian "work ethic" begins with God, the Creator, just as loving and thinking do. *As early as the creation narrative, God is put before us as a God who is at work.*[39] Martin Luther spoke of a *deus semper actuosus*, the unswervingly productive God. That mankind is to work for six days and is to rest on the seventh is founded in the Ten Commandments on the fact that God created the world in six days and after that he rested "from all his work" (Genesis 2:2). The Bible often speaks of God's work,[40] with the Psalmist speaking about "the works [or work] of your hands" (Psalm 138:8b). Man can sleep peacefully and rest can be taken from work, because "indeed, he who watches over Israel will neither slumber nor sleep" (Psalm 121:4).

With respect to the biblical work ethic,[41] work has such great dignity because it is founded in the image of God in mankind. We will see later that

---

[38] Ibid. p. 65.
[39] Comp. Dennis Peacocke. Almighty and Sons. Doing Business God's Way! Rebuild: Santa Rosa (CA), 1995. pp. 51-54.
[40] Comp. Horst Dietrich Preuß. "Arbeit I." pp. 613-618 in: Gerhard Müller (ed.). Theologische Realenzyklopädie. Vol. 3. de Gruyter: Berlin, 1993/1978 (Studienausgabe), here p. 614-615 (comp. everything regarding "Arbeit." pp. 613-669).
[41] Comp. Alfred de Quervain. Ruhe und Arbeit, Lohn und Eigentum. Ethik II Vol. 3. Evangelischer Verlag: Zollikon (CH), 1956. pp. 17-112+149-165; Miroslav Volf. "Arbeit, Geist und Schöpfung." pp. 32-60 in: Hermann Sautter, Miroslav Volf. Gerechtigkeit, Geist und Schöpfung: Die Oxford-Erklärung zur Frage von Glaube und Wirtschaft. Brockhaus: Wuppertal, 1992 and the good compilation by Derek Prime. Biblische Lebenshilfen im Grundriß. Verlag der Francke-Buchhandlung: Marburg, 1990. pp. 42-43, as well as the moderately critical study: Walther Bienert. Die Arbeit nach der Lehre der Bibel. Evangelisches Verlagswerk: Stuttgart, 1954 (pp. 414-428 comprehensive literature); Alan Richardson. Die biblische Lehre von der Arbeit. Anker-Verlag: Frankfurt, 1953; Udo Krolzik. Umweltkrise: Folge des Christentums? Kreuz Verlag: Stuttgart, 1979. pp. 61-70. The study which is most in line with our explanations regarding the work ethic is by Doug

anchoring work in God's activity as Creator has many practical consequences. Three of them have already been mentioned: 1) the more responsibility that is passed on to someone, the more work one has, 2) work is always shared work, which corresponds to respective giftings, and 3) work is always for each other.

The dignity of work

Work is thus a component of the image of God in man. If it is not beyond God to be at work, then all work has its dignity. Work is not in itself 'degrading' or 'dirty work.' Rather, it is a reflection of the creative activity of God. The ancient world saw this completely differently: "In Hellenism work was viewed as a fate cast upon mankind by the gods from which one could not escape. To live like God meant to live unburdened by work. In the old oriental environment, work was seen as a vice, as a service of slavery to the gods who were freed from labor. The goal was to elude this service or work as far as was possible. Work meant a burden without dignity."[42]

However, such a wrong view of work does not only exist in the extra-Christian realm, as above all the centuries before the Reformation show. "St. Thomas Aquinas [1224-1274] represented the view that the necessity to work is solely what compels. From that standpoint it is less than remarkable that the High Middle Ages saw the benefit of work in overcoming idleness, subduing the body, and producing a livelihood. Next to this a tendency can be recognized that assumed Greek thinking (chiefly Aristotelian) with an emphasis on the 'contemplative' and a disparagement of the 'active' life. Such it was that exemption from manual labor was legitimated for the knightly and priestly estates."[43]

Sherman; William Hendricks. Your Work Matters to God. NavPress: Colorado Springs (CO), 1990[Pb]; John Stott. Christsein in den Brennpunkten unserer Zeit ... 3 ... im sozialen Bereich. Francke: Marburg, 1988 [Engl. 1984]. pp. 11-64; Michael A. Zigarelli. Christianity 9 to 5: Living Your Faith at Work. Beacon Hill Press: Kansas City (MI), 1998; "Arbeit." pp. 189-204 in: Lexikon der Bioethik. 3 Vols. Vol. 1. Gütersloher Verlagshaus: Gütersloh, 1998; Walter Künneth. Moderne Wirtschaft – Christliche Existenz. Claudius: München, 1959. pp. 6-8, Abschnitt "Arbeit als Stiftung Gottes."

[42] Heiner Ruschhaupt. "Bauen und Bewahren." Der Navigator (Die Navigatoren: Bonn) No. 13 (May/June 1987): 2-3; comp. also Hans Frambach. Arbeit im ökonomischen Denken: Zum Wandel des Arbeitsverständnisses von der Antike bis zur Gegenwart. Metropolis Verlag: Marburg, 1999.

[43] Friedrich Trzaskalik. "Katholizismus." pp. 24-41 in: Michael Klöcker, Udo Tworuschka (ed.) . Ethik der Religionen – Lehre und Leben: Vol. 2: Arbeit. Kösel: München & Vandenhoeck & Ruprecht: Göttingen, 1985, here p. 33.

Hermann Cremer places the worldwide influence of the biblical ethic over against the aforementioned perspective. "It was not until Christianity, that is, the religion of revelation, that the world gained a different view of the nature and value of work. Classical antiquity assigned the execution of labor to those who were not free and were without rights. In doing so, antiquity caught sight of a decent existence by achieving emancipation from work, and it dishonored any work bound up with manual exertion."[44]

However, the biblical view, as we saw in our example, became increasingly obscured in the Catholic Middle Ages until the Reformation. "The Reformers such as Luther and Calvin were the first to begin to use the expressions of profession and *vocatio*[45] for the everyday tasks and lifetime post of an individual. It is important to note that they did this in protest against the limited medieval linguistic usage of exclusively applying the terms to the calling to a monastic life. They wanted to destroy the double moral standard and show that God could also be glorified in the daily work world."[46] "Martin Luther had – and herein lies one of his transvaluation of values, from which effects went far beyond Protestantism and the religious sphere – ennobled work and had made it holy. This also applied to work that had to do with money making. It is through Luther that in German the word *Berufung* [calling] was modified to a theretofore unknown concept of *Beruf* [occupation]."[47]

Protestant global missions also particularly spread this work ethic around the world. The "father of missiology," Gustav Warneck, wrote in this connection: "... Christian mission shows with word and example that work branded with the shame of slavery rests upon a divine command ..."[48]

Work in the Garden of Eden

The "Garden of Eden" was no paradise in the sense that there was work associated with it. Adam and Eve had to plant in order to produce food,

---

[44] Hermann Cremer. Arbeit und Eigentum in christlicher Sicht. Brunnen Verlag: Gießen, 1984. p. 8.
[45] Latin for profession/calling.
[46] Alan Richardson. Die biblische Lehre von der Arbeit. op. cit. p. 27 (sic).
[47] Gerhard Simon. "Bibel und Börse: Die religiösen Wurzeln des Kapitalismus." Archiv für Kulturgeschichte 66 (1984): 87-115, here p. 101; comp. Paul Althaus. Die Ethik Martin Luthers. Gütersloher Verlagshaus: Gütersloh, 1965^1. pp. 105-108.
[48] Gustav Warneck. Die Stellung der evangelischen Mission zur Sklavenfrage. C. Bertelsmann: Gütersloh,1889. p. 67.

and all animals had to be given names. Work had to be done (Genesis 1:26-30, esp. 28-29; 2:8, 11-12, 15, 19-20). In Genesis 2:15 man receives the task of *working* the earth and *taking* care of it. Change and preservation are the two aspects of all work. Work is not "the consequence of and punishment for sin. It is the difficulties and failings associated with work, according to the unanimous interpretation of Jewish expositors of Genesis 3:17-19, that are in contrast to the carefree and effortless nature of paradise. As a result, in Judaism manual labor does not receive the disdain that it does from the Greeks and the Romans." [49]

Hermann Cremer sees the situation similarly: "It is not work itself, but rather the imbalance between work and success or returns, that is to say, burden and hardship in relation to success that is the consequence of sin."[50]

In the new heavens and the new earth (comp. Isaiah 65:17-25), work will no longer be in vain, but work will still be conducted: "They will build houses and dwell in them; they will plant vineyards and eat their fruit. No longer will they build houses and others live in them, or plant and others eat ... my chosen ones will long enjoy the works of their hands. They will not toil in vain or bear children doomed to misfortune; for they will be a people blessed by the Lord, they and their descendants with them" (Isaiah 65:21-23).

Even eternal paradise with God will not be a paradise as some think of it. It will be filled with praise and service to God. This is in contrast to Islam, where men lie upon beds and eat and drink while being served by beautiful women. Islam knows neither of an Adam who worked in paradise, nor of work that is not under a curse, nor of service in heaven.[51]

Whoever wants to achieve or receive something good has to invest work. The 'good works' that are often recommended and desired in the Bible are, according to the Greek term that is used, actually refer to 'good work.' And, as Erich Kästner said, "Nothing is good unless someone does it!"

---

[49] Johannes Wachten. "Judentum." pp. 9-23 in: Michael Klöcker, Udo Tworuschka (ed.) . Ethik der Religionen – Lehre und Leben: Vol. 2: Arbeit. Kösel: München; Vandenhoeck & Ruprecht: Göttingen, 1985, here p. 10. Leo Baeck. Das Wesen des Judentums. Fourier: Wiesbaden, 1991⁵ (Nachdruck von 1921²). p. 221 schreibt: "Das Judentum lehrt den Segen der Arbeit ... Für das Judentum gehört die Arbeit zum Menschsein."

[50] Hermann Cremer. Arbeit und Eigentum in christlicher Sicht. op. cit. p. 9.

[51] Cf.. Monika Tworuschka. "Islam." pp. 64-84 in: Michael Klöcker, Udo Tworuschka (ed.). Ethik der Religionen – Lehre und Leben. Vol. 2: Arbeit. op. cit. p. 67, 69.

1. Loving, thinking, working

Example from family life

> Whenever you get to know a married couple that has been happily married for a long time, you will quickly recognize that no good relationship simply falls into one's lap. Instead of that, such a couple has 'invested' time and work. The couple has taken time for each other, addressed problems, and discussed things thoroughly. A way has been worked out that gives the relationship a priority over other work (e.g., professional occupation or children). The relationship has also been tended to, often by utilizing the help of friends and counselors. "From nothing nothing comes." This also applies to marriage. True love never comes via idleness. Rather, "let us not love with words or tongue but with actions and in truth" (1 John 3:18).

The value of work

Work itself is of value in the Bible, regardless of whether one is paid for it or not. After all, the stipulation is the following: "… for the worker deserves his wages" (Luke 10:7; 1 Corinthians 9:9; comp. Deuteronomy 25:4). Jeremiah 22:13 shows how seriously the Bible takes payment for work: "Woe to him who builds his palace by unrighteousness, his upper rooms by injustice, making his countrymen work for nothing, not paying them for their labor."

The statement that "the worker deserves his wages" makes every type of work worthwhile and expresses an obligation to pay fairly, which should not be withheld in any circumstances (Matthew 10:10; Deuteronomy 24:14; Leviticus 19:13). The commandment is understood in the New Testament to be an obligation of the church towards its elders (1 Timothy 5:17-18) as well as a basic criticism of entrepreneurs and materialism: "Look! The wages you failed to pay the workmen who mowed your fields are crying out against you. The cries of the harvesters have reached the ears of the Lord Almighty" (James 5:4).

Work is not only valuable when compensation is received. Rather, work is to be paid for fairly because it has a value in and of itself. On account of this, compensated and non-compensated work have the same significance. If man is supposed to work six days, that does not implicitly mean that he should work six days for money. If one counts what is listed as the tasks of a woman in Proverbs 31:11-31, it is amazing what sort of variety appears there and how such diverse activities, whether they bring in money or not, are placed side by side.

This certainly includes the idea that each person is supposed to work according to his or her abilities and insofar as is possible. Work is not a neutral part of the order of nature, that is to say, it is not a necessity in itself.

Rather, God wills that there be work, because one finds a correspondence to him who has ordered the creation.

The Ten Commandments contain the commandment "six days you shall labor and do all your work" (Exodus 20:8-10; Deuteronomy 5:12-15), which does not automatically mean a six-day time period of compensated work. This commandment is in fact also fulfilled by the housewife, by voluntary social work, or other unsalaried work. Due to this, in the Bible laziness is sin. "One of the most bitter denouncements of the prophets has to do with the lazy rich (e.g., Amos 6:3-6)."[52] Wealth can be something positive and something that is enjoyed. This is not the case, however, if it becomes one's principle purpose in life or if wealth displaces or even destroys the benefits it can bring.

Authority means work

God is a God who works more than any member of mankind, because he has more authority than all of mankind. He does not "slumber nor sleep" (Psalm 121:4b).

Accordingly, responsibility and power bring additional work. Among the religions, it is a distinctive feature of Christianity (and Judaism) that responsibility and authority lead to more work. The authority that mankind has over the earth (Genesis 1:26-30) as the "crown of creation," that is to say, the task of tending to and caring for the earth, is tantamount to the mandate to work and to maintain the earth. This means not only to alter ("cultivate") but also to preserve ("safeguard"), as Genesis 2:15 makes clear: "The Lord God took the man and put him in the Garden of Eden to work it and take care of it."

Example from the state sector

> The mandate to work is also specifically for the powerful. Kings lead a particularly hardworking life in the Bible, much as a chancellor or a cabinet minister would today. In a culture influenced by Christianity, the German Chancellor would be voted out of office very quickly if he spends one-half of the year on vacation and more time on the island of Mallorca than in the capital.

Example from church life

> Authority is often founded on the basis of the work that superiors conduct for their subordinates. In 1 Corinthians 16: 15b-16 the following is said of

---

[52] Alan Richardson. Die biblische Lehre von der Arbeit. op. cit. p. 16.

those who carry responsibility in the church: "... they have devoted themselves to the service of the saints. I urge you, brothers, to submit to such as these and to everyone who joins in the work, and labors at it." Paul, who was certainly not without influence, also wrote, "I worked harder than all of them" (1 Corinthians 15:10; 2 Corinthians 11:23). Work was the price for his responsibility. In the Bible those who have higher positions work for their subordinates as much as the subordinates work for them. Parents work for their children, and 'breadwinners' work for their families. Authority means work in the Bible, whereby the highest authority, God himself, does more for us than we could do for each other.

Example from family life

The authority that parents have for their children does not secure a comfortable life for parents; rather, it calls for a lot of work.

It is astounding to see how the work ethic stands in close relationship to respective religions and concepts of God. Buddha is the paragon of a god who does not work, for the very reason that he is god. He lets himself be served, and everyone can see in his external appearance where this leads. Buddhism aligns its work ethic with its concept of god. Buddha, who does not work, who relaxes and becomes fat from his rest and from his gifts, molds an objective for those who believe in him. The Buddhist monk's ideal underscores this. Buddhism does not have a word for work,[53] and work is not a topic in Buddhist ethics.[54] Buddhism and socialism have a lot in common when it comes to the questions of work and the economy, and numerous Buddhist authors have highlighted this.[55]

Example from the state sector

In many other religions and cultures there is a phrase that having power means not having to work. There were also absolutist rulers in Europe who conducted their affairs of state while on the toilet. And apart from that they amused themselves with wine, women, and song at the expense of the people.

---

[53] Comp . Peter Gerlitz. "Buddhismus." pp. 100-118 in: Michael Klöcker, Udo Tworuschka (ed.). Ethik der Religionen – Lehre und Leben. Vol. 2: Arbeit. Kösel: München, Vandenhoeck & Ruprecht: Göttingen, 1985, p. 101.

[54] Ibid.

[55] Comp. ibid. pp. 112-115.

The divine and human division of labor

Within the divine Trinity, all planning and activity are questions of a division of labor. The persons of the Trinity love each other, speak with each other, and do things for each other. Only in the case of a division of labor can one person serve another. The diversity of spiritual gifts makes this clear for the church. And this diversity goes back to the division of labor in the Trinity.

Example from family life

> The family is the best example of division of labor, which is the reason Karl Marx was right when he practically equated the division of labor with marriage and the family. Man and woman received different duties from God and divide the labor, which makes up a significant element of marriage. The unity in diversity applies in marriage as it does everywhere where there is work, whether that is in the family, the church, the economy, the culture, or the state.

Limiting work: work and rest

As much as man was created to work,[56] work in the Bible always has its limits. The division of labor is one of the many reasons for this. Man should not "overwork" and become engulfed in his labor. One could also formulate it as follows: work in the Bible is never an end in itself. Rather, it always receives second place after God and his righteousness (comp. Matthew 6:33). This is the sense of the seventh day as a day of rest. Man reminds himself that he can only work "the six working days" (Ezekiel 46:1), because the Creator made him and because God placed the creation at his disposal.

Helmut Thielicke aptly stated that the biblical understanding of work lies "between the ancient Greek devaluation of work and the modern idealized glorification of it."[57] Work should fill our life, but it is not the final and all-deciding factor.

---

[56] Indeed the connection between unemployment and a higher suicide rate, which is often used to support the idea that man was created to work, is presumably unfounded; comp. "Kein Zusammenhang zwischen Suizid und Arbeitslosigkeit." Deutsches Ärzteblatt 87 (1990) No. 31/32 (August 6, 1990): p. A-2411 as a summary by I. K. Crombie. "Trends in Suicide and Unemployment in Scotland 1976-86." British Medical Journal 298 (1987): 782-784.

[57] Helmut Thielicke. Theologische Ethik. Vol. 2. Part 1: Mensch und Welt. J. C. B. Mohr: Tübingen, 1959.² pp. 396-397.

Example from family life

> Each working person knows how difficult it can be to reconcile work, marriage, and family. As a general rule, a marriage partner generally knows whether work has become an end in itself and has taken on the highest value, while it should basically be subordinated to one's partner and one's family. This does not necessarily have to do with the amount of work or time management. Does your child know that his problems have priority over all the problems of the world? Or does your child have to take drugs before you take time for him or her? Does your marriage partner know that his or her problems will be taken just as seriously as those of your boss or your company? Are you just as creative in solving the problems of your family as you are in solving economic problems?[58]

A Japanese association of lawyers figures that in Japan 10,000 people die annually from overwork.[59] 'Death by overworking' has been officially recognized by the Japanese Ministry of Labor as a cause of death. It has its own name in Japanese (*karoshi*) and mostly arises from an excess of overtime hours and a lack of relaxation. "Home simply becomes a place to sleep."[60]

God as an Employer: without God there is no work

The seventh day is there to remind man that without God he could not truly work and that all his work would essentially be in vain. This also applies generally: "Unless the Lord builds the house, its builders labor in vain. Unless the Lord watches over the city, the watchmen stand guard in vain. In vain you rise early and stay up late, toiling for food to eat – for he grants sleep to those he loves" (Psalm 127:1-2). Proverbs 10:22 says it more succinctly: "The blessing of the LORD brings wealth, and he adds no trouble to it" (comp Matthew 6:24-34). When Jesus says to his disciples, "… apart from me you can do nothing" (John 15:15), he is not only referring to 'spiritual' questions. Without God no one is able to do anything. The first people in paradise were only able to conduct activity because God planted a garden for them and gave them many skills.

---

[58] Comp. from a secular viewpoint the excellent book by Günter F. Gross. Beruflich Profi, privat Amateur? Berufliche Spitzenleistungen und persönliche Lebensqualität. verlag moderne industrie: Landsberg, 1996.[13]

[59] "Feierabend für Japans Wegwerfarbeiter?" Die Welt No. 147 dated June 26, 1992. p. 3; D. P. "Zu Tode gearbeitet." Der Kassenarzt 12/1991: 32.

[60] Ibid.

According to Exodus 31:2-6 and 35:31, artists could only build the tabernacle because God had given them the technical skills. On account of this there is an inseparable connection between gratitude towards God and work. In Isaiah 28:23-29 it is said that the success a farmer has in plowing, sowing, planting, maturing, threshing, milling, and baking bread goes back to God's instructions."[61] "His God instructs him and teaches him the right way" (Isaiah 28:26).[62]

That work is given by God and is to be subordinated to God is not only expressed in the notion of the day of rest. In the Old Testament the Israelites gave their first born and the tithe to God and testified with this that God had enabled them to work. Gustav Friedrich Oehler points out in this connection that when it came to the "things for sacrifice" that people brought, it had to do "with regular foodstuffs produced by the people in the course of their labors,"[63] just as was clearly the case with the first sacrifices of Cain and Abel. Here also a demonstration of the close relationship between work and worship is expressed.

Work for God

So understood, in the final event work is done not for the worker himself, nor for his family, nor for a human employer, but instead, in the truest sense of the word, it is done for God: "And whatever you do, whether in word or deed, do it all in the name of the Lord Jesus, giving thanks to God the Father through him" (Colossians 3:17). "Whatever you do, work at it with all your heart, as working for the Lord, not for men, [24]since you know that you will receive an inheritance from the Lord as a reward. It is the Lord Christ you are serving" (Colossians 3:23-24). These verses are not to be limited to religious activities, because the wording is: "Whatever you do, ..."

"The nobleness of work no longer flows from its 'what' but from its 'why.' Through the charge to serve God and through the relevance it has to one's neighbor, the slightest physical labor is as valuable as that which is 'intellectual.'"[64]

Many have taken offense from the fact that the Bible directs slaves to work particularly well and honestly toward their masters (Titus 2:9-11;

---

[61] Alan Richardson. Die biblische Lehre von der Arbeit. op. cit., p. 15.
[62] Comp. the detailed description of work in context.
[63] Gustav Friedrich Oehler. Theologie des Alten Testaments. J. F. Steinkopf: Stuttgart, 1891.³ p. 437.
[64] Emil Brunner. Das Gebot und die Ordnungen. Zwingli Verlag: Zürich, 1939.⁴ p. 373.

Ephesians 6:5-9; Colossians 3:22-4:1; 1 Timothy 6:1-2; 1 Peter 2:18-25; 1 Corinthians 7:21-24). The grounds for this, however, are important: "… not only when their eye is on you and to win their favor, but with sincerity of heart and reverence for the Lord. Whatever you do, work at it with all your heart, as working for the Lord, not for men" (Colossians 3:22-23). It is not the one who pays the wages who is the underlying employer; rather, it is God. The Christian slave knows that his work is good and dignified in the sight of God.

It is only after taking these basic attitudes into account that strong admonitions are directed towards employers, in which they are reminded of their legal obligations. This is on account of the fact that God does not look at the standing a person has.

The same Paul who encourages slaves to work well and to prove oneself a Christian as a slave, is able to write, "Each one should remain in the situation which he was in when God called him. Were you a slave when you were called? Don't let it trouble you – although if you can gain your freedom, do so. For he who was a slave when he was called by the Lord is the Lord's freedman; similarly, he who was a free man when he was called is Christ's slave" (1 Corinthians 7:20-22). In Philemon Paul vehemently becomes involved in an effort to emancipate a slave. Is that a contradiction to the texts in which Paul calls upon slaves to be obedient? Not at all. According to the Bible every person is a slave of sin and is caught in rebellion against God. If he accepts this judgment by God as well as the substitutionary, sacrificial death of Jesus, he is someone who is called by God. Forgiveness of sins frees the individual to new life. For this new life it is not necessary that every personal circumstance immediately change for the better. Just as in the case of other addicts (who are enslaved), such a person can serve God lock, stock, and barrel.

This has nothing to do with the question of whether one should tolerate slavery or even endorse it. Paul recommends that the slave be set free and advocates this emphatically ("… although if you can gain your freedom, do so", v. 21b). Notice that faith in God places all other values in a new light. It is not work as such that makes life valuable, but rather the Creator and Redeemer who entrusts us with work. The persuasive power of Christianity is found in the fact that under the call to seek God's righteousness, righteousness is commanded and promoted in all bluntness. But even when righteousness is denied, thankfulness towards God remains, and the believer is not dependent on external circumstances in order to practice righteousness.

Work for others

Work is never work solely for the one working. Rather, it is also always work for another. Work is service.

For one thing, work is itself a service to others. Our language, under Christian influence, has retained in manifold ways the notion that work is a service. The Latin word *minister* is the Latin word for "servant," just as we see in the designation "public service"[65] which includes all public offices held. We also refer to a "service" being provided and to the "service sector."[66]

On the other hand, the proceeds of work do not go solely to the worker. Paul writes, "Command those who are rich in this present world not to be arrogant nor to put their hope in wealth, which is so uncertain, but to put their hope in God, who richly provides us with everything for our enjoyment. Command them to do good, to be rich in good deeds, and to be generous and willing to share. In this way they will lay up treasure for themselves as a firm foundation for the coming age, so that they may take hold of the life that is truly life" (1 Timothy 6:17-19). Wealth should serve one's own enjoyment as well as serve others, whereby service to others inures in heaven to the one who provides the service. "The New Testament does not fail to recognize that work should serve to sustain one's own life (Ephesians 4:28; 1 Thessalonians 4:11; 2 Thessalonians 3:8, 12). But even after this aspect is taken into account, the proceeds of work are not just for the one who performed it."[67]

A fixed portion – in the Old Testament the tithe – belongs to God, and a further portion belongs to the state community. In addition thereto, providing for one's own family is also commanded (1 Timothy 5:8). For Christians this applies additionally to social responsibilities within the Christian church as well as global efforts in missions and social welfare work. Paul requests that a thief who until now has lived at the expense of others should now live as a Christian to help others: "He who has been stealing must steal no longer, but must work, doing something useful with his own hands, that he may have something to share with those in need" (Ephesians 4:28).

As has so often been the case, we have to look at two sides at this point. On the one hand, work takes place for the sake of providing for oneself. On the other hand, work serves others, be it that work occurs directly for them

---

[65] Comp. Alan Richardson. Die biblische Lehre von der Arbeit. op. cit. p. 44-45.

[66] As good as this concept is, it should not convey that no 'service is offered' in other sectors of the economy.

[67] Hermann Cremer. Arbeit und Eigentum in christlicher Sicht. op. cit. p. 11.

(e.g., the work of a bus driver), or be it that the end product of work produces something useful (e.g., a baby carriage), or be it that the working person gives some of his wages away (e.g., providing for his family). John Stott calls this the "biblical principle of reciprocity."[68] Neither side should be played off against the other. A secular economist writes in a manner that demonstrates an understanding of the biblical connections that entangle many Christians: "The belief that the happiness of another person benefits oneself only finds its way with difficulty to the human heart. However, this is the golden rule of economics, the key to peace and affluence, and a precondition for progress."[69]

How can this be conveyed to a secular environment?
The dignity of man does not arise from his work. On the contrary, mankind's dignity precedes him and even applies to people who are unable to work, e.g., a baby. A person should not merge with his work and build his entire life on it. In fact, he should have a more comprehensive and holistic canon of values, which in our tradition is above all expressed in a Sunday that is free from work. Still, under normal circumstances, the dignity of man automatically leads to the fact that every person contributes via his work to shape the world, to be there for each other, and in that way to enable us to live together. This means fulfillment for the individual, who wants to change and plan in contrast to an animal which takes everything instinctually. This also, however, means life for others. The individual can only exist because many others are directly or indirectly active and produce the conditions for a dignified life, the shoemaker, who makes good footwear, as well as the policeman who protects him, or the doctor who cures him.

The burden of work

To a certain degree what follows is the negative side of work. In connection with the fall of man, the soil is cursed (Genesis 3:17-19; 5:29), and the result is that work becomes arduous and painstaking. In addition to successes and benefits, there are again and again failures and disintegration ("thorns and thistles"). Man thought that as the crown of creation he was able to possess a dignity in work, but he also thought he was able to simultaneously disregard the giver of all work and creation. Since that time, the arduousness and burden of work reminds every person on a daily basis that his or her relationship to God has been destroyed. Whoever wishes "para-

---

[68] John Stott. Christsein in den Brennpunkten unserer Zeit ... 3. op. cit. p. 38-42.
[69] George Gilder. Reichtum und Armut. op. cit. p. 19.

disiacal" work for himself denies the fall of man and its consequences, because toilsome work is also assigned to us by God: "What does the worker gain from his toil? I have seen the burden God has laid on men (Ecclesiastes 3:10).

After all, the composer of the book of Ecclesiastes does not draw the conclusion that man should rather not work, but rather that all the more – in spite of all the toil – one may and should rejoice in the beautiful things: "I know that there is nothing better for men than to be happy and do good while they live. That everyone may eat and drink, and find satisfaction in all his toil – this is the gift of God" (Ecclesiastes 3:12-13).

The Bible summons us to take this daily toil upon ourselves. Whoever steals or lives at the expense of others is only shifting the toil to others, which the following statement from the Apostle Paul demonstrates: "For you yourselves know how you ought to follow our example. We were not idle when we were with you, nor did we eat anyone's food without paying for it. On the contrary, we worked night and day, laboring and toiling so that we would not be a burden to any of you" (2 Thessalonians 3:7-8).

Additional examples from the letters of Paul reveal that every Christian should carry his own burden: "Yet we urge you, brothers, to do so more and more. Make it your ambition to lead a quiet life, to mind your own business and to work with your hands, just as we told you, so that your daily life may win the respect of outsiders and so that you will not be dependent on anybody" (1 Thessalonians 4:10-12. "For even when we were with you, we gave you this rule: 'If a man will not work, he shall not eat.' We hear that some among you are idle. They are not busy; they are busybodies. Such people we command and urge in the Lord Jesus Christ to settle down and earn the bread they eat. And as for you, brothers, never tire of doing what is right" (2 Thessalonians 3:10-13).

This does not mean that an individual is not allowed to use his or her own work to support someone else who does not have work. On the contrary, the thief who has until now lived at the expense of others is asked to help others: "He who has been stealing must steal no longer, but must work, doing something useful with his own hands, that he may have something to share with those in need" (Ephesians 4:28). That a former thief should care for himself is not specifically mentioned because it is tacitly assumed. The bottom line is that someone who was a thief now works for others.

Basil the Great[70] (approx. 329-379 A.D.), with recourse to 2 Thessalonians, described the Christian work ethic when he pointed out that work also has as an object to care for the poor.

1.4. The three aspects of every decision

Therefore, we are now attuned to the idea to love, to think, and to work when we make decisions.

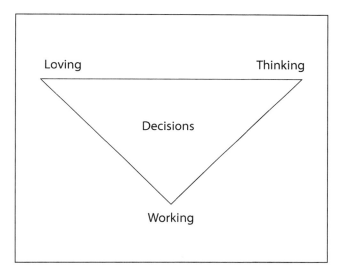

In the following we want to consecutively look at three aspects of each decision, in particular of each decision made as a leader.

The normative aspect's importance is expressed in God's unchanging **commandments**. In ethics we generally find the normative aspect in basic values.

The situational aspect's importance is expressed in **wisdom**, which gauges situations on the basis of experience and specific situations. In ethics a so-called collision of obligations, a situational ethic, and cultural assimilation all play a role.

---

[70] Basilius der Große. 'Ausführliche Regeln' 41, 1-2, abgedruckt in Alfons Heilmann (ed.). Texte der Kirchenväter. 5 vols. Vol. 3. Kösel: München, 1964. pp. 228-229; comp. ibid. pp. 224-240 numerous texts by Church Fathers on the Christian view of work. Comp. Adolf von Harnack regarding the position of the early church on work. Die Mission und Ausbreitung des Christentums in den ersten drei Jahrhunderten. VMA-Verlag: Wiesbaden, o. J. (1924[4] Reprint). pp. 197-200.

The existential aspect's importance is expressed in the meaning of the **heart** and the **conscience**, whereby in the individual the actual decision is made on the basis of normative and situational considerations. At this point in ethics, one generally speaks about the conscience and motives.

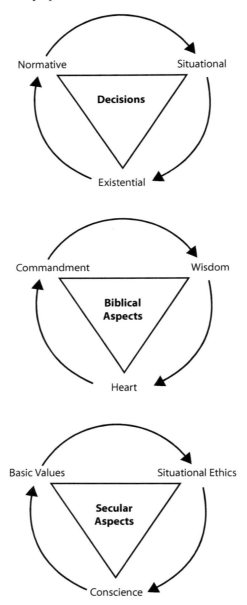

Normative, situational, and existential aspects are classical ethical blueprints. They assume that via norms and commandments it is predefined how mankind is supposed to act, but that only in a particular situation is an individual able to grasp what the best thing is. Alternatively, the ethical decision takes place within us as a struggle having to do with our existence.

I consider all three aspects to be incorrect if they stand alone and are played off against each other. I consider all three aspects as legitimate if they are understood as important links in an overall decision. Above all I am of the opinion that all three aspects are widely testified to in the Bible and that they are seen as complementary and not in opposition to each other.[71]

When in the following I assign different focuses to these aspects, it is not to be understood that a perfect boundary is possible. This applies in particular to the many examples. Since every decision contains all three aspects, one could present most examples under other categories, but I particularly emphasize one aspect in each case.

2. Normative decisions

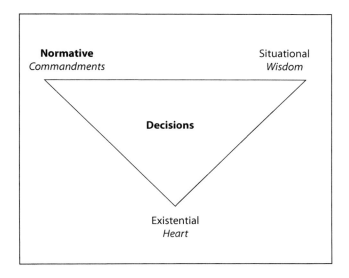

---

[71] So also in John M. Frame. Perspectives on the Word of God: An Introduction to Christian Ethics. Wipf and Stock Publ.: Eugene (OR), 1999²; Presbyterian and Reformed Publ.: Phillipsburg (NJ), 1990¹. pp. 51-56.

2.1. Leading normatively means setting values and drawing boundaries

Values and faith

"No human community can get along without norms, because man (in contrast to an animal, which is driven by instinct) does not know simply as a matter of nature how to behave in a way that leads to a functioning community."[72]

At this point we should really repeat what was said at the beginning about love and the relationship of love to commandments and values. If necessary, the section on love should be skimmed over again.

The significance of values and norms is determined by love. They presuppose a readiness to defend them out of love and to draw boundaries where these values are trampled underfoot. These values are not just givens, and they are not able to just be ascertained anywhere or proved by scientific research. On the contrary, they arise out of each person's beliefs and faith, and 'belief' and 'faith' in this context are not meant to be understood in a precise sense. Rather, they encompass everything upon which a person trusts in without being able to prove it in advance.

The significance that belief and faith have for values does not mean, however, that these values are divested of reflection, because the implications of such basic decisions can very well be scrutinized in actual life.

Are there people who have no ethics?

"All human thought and action is connected with a worldview. Everyone integrates himself and his action into the framework of a comprehensive meaning of mankind and the world, within which an individual's behavior first has its meaning."[73]

This statement and the quotation at the beginning of the chapter tellingly stem from the pens of a lawyer and a scientist, not from a theologian. When nowadays firm believers in Christianity present their conception of morality, they are often only answered with a smirk. Using the Bible as a benchmark for moral and ethical action? Should such antiquated ideas of

---

[72] Andreas Henrici. "Das schweizerische Recht." pp. 365-369 in: Niklaus Flüeler; Roland Gfeller-Corthésy. Die Schweiz. Ex Libris Verlag/Migros: op. cit., 1975, here p. 365.

[73] Hansjörg Hemminger. Psychotherapie: Weg zum Glück? Zur Orientierung auf dem Psychomarkt. Münchener Reihe. Evangelischer Presseverband für Bayern: München, 1987. p. 5.

2. Normative decisions

what is good and bad still find any validity in our day and age? Are ethics only a thing for Christians and other world religions? Surely not, as the following atheistic definition of ethics shows: "Ethics: moral doctrine, an area of philosophy which investigates mores and morals, i.e., the moral practices, values, norms and views of people as well as the principles of moral development and has the task of developing and justifying moral values in accordance with objective societal requirements."[74]

This foregoing definition does not come from a 'religious' book, but rather out of the *Dictionary of Marxist-Leninist Philosophy* from what used to be the German Democratic Republic. For millennia Ethics has been a domain of philosophy. Whoever studies philosophy at university has to take courses and seminars in ethics. Whoever looks at a history of ethics book will most probably find that he is looking at a history of philosophy book.[75] Almost all well known philosophers up to the present age also developed an ethic.[76] Many a philosopher, for example Immanuel Kant, has gone down into history for their ethical systems. The philosophical-ethical system of the neo-Marxist and so-called 'Frankfurt School'[77] (Adorno, Horkheimer, Habermas, Marcuse) gained influence in educational policy and in legislation in the Federal Republic of Germany. It is probably the prior philosophical history that is the reason why many leaders see ethics today as something that is highly theoretical and dry and has its own distinct language for insiders.

A similar thing to what one sees in ethics also applies to other subjects. In the school of medicine, medical ethics is taught; modern educational science has at its base ideas about the ethical goals of upbringing; psychology is always proposing new value systems as a matter of course, and it eagerly puts these before its clients; and last but not least, schools of law uninterruptedly address ethical decisions, specifically in the area of 'legal doctrine,' which sets the foundation for jurisprudence and works out which values should be protected.

---

[74] Alfred Kosing. Wörterbuch der marxistisch-leninistischen Philosophie. Dietz: (Ost-)Berlin, 1986². p. 166.

[75] Z. B. Friedrich Jodl. Geschichte der Ethik. 2 vols. Magnus-Verlag: Essen, 1982 (Vol. 1 reprint: 1929⁴; Vol. 2: 1923³); particularly interesting on the alleged scientific ethics of evolution: Vol. 2. p. 455ff.

[76] Comp. the selection in Karl-Otto Apel, Gerhard Plumpe. Praktische Philosophie/Ethik. Vol 1. Aktuelle Materialien zum Funk-Kolleg. Fischer Taschenbuch Verlag: Frankfurt, 1980.

[77] Comp. to Jacob Klapwijk's presentation and critique. Philosophische Kritik und göttliche Offenbarung. Fundamentum. Immanuel-Verlag: Riehen, 1991.

While philosophers, physicians, educators, psychologists, and many other scientists including liberal theologians pursue and disseminate their 'scientific' forms of ethics (not to mention the innumerable versions of ethics outside the university), and millions of people act in accordance with their varied standards, firm believers in Christianity often have to put up with being disparaged as people from the backwoods, die-hards, and gadflies. In the process one forgets all too easily that there is actually no single person who lives or could live without a conscious or subconscious form of ethics.

Sources of vvangelical ethics

As far as normative decisions and values are concerned, the question is posed as to where Christian leaders take these values and upon which basis then have their authority. Alister McGrath writes in this connection: "Loosely speaking, the Christian tradition has recognized four main sources: 1. the Holy Scriptures, 2. Reason, 3. Tradition, 4. Experience."[78]

Next to this one could point out the situation (the actual circumstances) as well as the respective culture surrounding us, and these factors can all be subsumed under the four classical sources named by McGrath. For evangelical ethics it is God's word, in the form of the Holy Scriptures, that is the sole rule, the guideline, against which all other authorities are to be measured (*norma normans*, that is, the norm for normalizing other norms). Due to the fact that God, as the Creator of the world, has throughout salvation history revealed himself, and because the most important things have been recorded in the Holy Scriptures for his creatures, every ethical thought for Christians begins upon the foundation of the Bible.

The question immediately arises about the significance of other factors, such as tradition, reason, wisdom, and experience, as well as the concrete situation and culture. Are they to be discarded because the Holy Scriptures are the highest authority, or may they be incorporated into ethical decisions? Naming tradition, experience, reason, and the situation (or culture) should not be tantamount to the naming the final sources and ways of knowledge. Rather, they are meant to express the classic designations in our cultural history with which we describe and in which manner good and correct insights are achieved.

---

[78] Alister E. McGrath. Der Weg der christlichen Theologie. C. H. Beck: München, 1997. p. 189; comp. more comprehensive ibid. p. 189-243 (Chapter 6: "Die Quellen der Theologie." The roles of reason and experience along side of scripture is discussed by Martin Honecker. Einführung in die Theologische Ethik. Walter de Gruyter: Berlin, 1990. pp. 187-202.

2. Normative decisions

One allegedly and particularly godly view seeks to exclude all of these factors from ethics. Ostensibly one can orient himself exclusively towards the Bible and throw out all other standards and words of advice. And naturally, one can simply refer to the fact that in reality such an approach is not at all possible. There is no one who exclusively "lives based on the Bible," and there is no one who is not able to decide *for* the good and *against* the bad when a situation is not directly illuminated by the Bible. In this way one can indeed compile arguments against smoking, even if the Bible never directly addresses the issue. Because of that, smoking is not clearly identified as a sin but is 'only' unhealthy, antisocial, and unwise.

At this point I would like to point out that such an exclusive concept is completely foreign to the Bible. In addition to divine revelation, the Bible repeatedly calls upon us to take the wisdom, experience, and pointers from various sources of authority, as well as the teachings from history, seriously. Furthermore, time and again in the Holy Scriptures there is reasoning that occurs on the basis of the experience of previous generations and by utilizing syllogisms. If the Bible is the highest authority, one has to admit that it is correct when it calls upon us to use advice, wisdom, experience, and reason and to take parental, church, economic, and state authorities seriously.

In this connection one can name the decisions made by lawful authorities such as parents, employers, church, and state. The meaning of these authorities is precisely such that they do not (or not only) guarantee compliance to divine commands or basic values, but that regulations are naturally set for our day and age that are not directly derived from God's word. Whoever is entitled to pass such laws, to determine to whom these laws apply and which areas such laws stake off, is surely active in regulating creation ordinances, upon which basic values rest. The authority to pass laws applying to certain people and for certain times 1. arises out of creation ordinances, 2. is only acceptable for the conferred area of responsibility, and 3. is never to lead to binding ordinances. But that does not change the fact that present traffic regulations, as a protection of life and as a way to regulate community life, are a component of Christian ethics, even if the Bible says nothing about driving nor regulates anything similar in any sort of detail.

God's revelation should be the starting point for our thinking, but it should not replace our thinking and planning. "The fear of the Lord is the *beginning* [author's emphasis] of wisdom" (Proverbs 9:10; similarly Proverbs 1:7), not the *end* of wisdom.

Example from family life

Can a child only be raised on the basis of the Bible? Naturally this is not the case, because the Bible says nothing about how one addresses health problems children may have, how long they should sleep, and which social graces are appropriate for children to acquire. The Bible also has nothing to say about when a child should be sent to school or about allowance money, to name just a few. However, the Bible does give us the divine significance and the basic direction of raising children. In this way child rearing that is tied to the Bible is different from all other types of child rearing that quickly takes recourse to 'recipes.' Parents should raise their children "in the training [*paideia*] and instruction [*nouthesia*] of the Lord" (Ephesians 6:4). They should make God and his word winsome (2 Timothy 3:14-17) and prepare them to live an independent life within the framework of the creation ordinances. Beyond such basic direction there are only occasionally individual commands or tips on child rearing, for instance, things that have to do with punishment and with passing on biblical stories.[79] If the biblical mandate to raise children is basically accepted, parents will of course simply derive much from the 'nature' of things in an environment created by God. Growth, which is to say, the physical and intellectual development of a child, forces a lot of decisions to be made compared with those made for other children. Additionally, this development in children can by all means be aptly and helpfully described by non-Christians. By the way, Christian parents are called to put this basic direction of child rearing into practice in everyday life with the aid of the Bible. For this they draw upon the experience of former generations (tradition) as well as upon advice and research from the present. They endeavor with all strength (emotional, intellectual, and financial) to find the best possible way for their children. Without knowing the children's concrete life situations, that would be impossible. After all, one has to know the culture in which one lives and, for example, the actual family constellation or the respective residential environment.

An additional example

It is God's desire and command that every person employs the abilities and gifts given to him by God. But how are parents to put this all into practice other than to use their reason and by observing and learning from others which talents, abilities, and proclivities children have so that they can be fostered in them? God has indeed provided a basic goal for raising children, but otherwise he has equipped mankind with reason and wisdom to find the best path for children.

---

[79] E.g., with respect to the law: Deuteronomy 4:9-10; 6:4-9, 20-25; 11:18-21; 31:12-13; 32:7; Joshua 4:6-7; Psalm 78:5-8; Proverbs 28:7; with respect to the Passover: Exodus 12:26-27; 13:14-16 [comp. 6-10].

At the so-called Council at Jerusalem there are numerous factors that played a role in serving as ethical sources with respect to a final decision: 1. the Holy Scriptures remained decisive (Acts 15: 15-19) and yet the following factors played secondary roles: 2. Peter's, Paul's and Barnabas' calling and concrete experience (Acts 15: 7-9, 12,14); 3. reasonable argumentation; 4. church authority. All levels of the church decided together: James as the head of the church in Jerusalem, the Apostles, missionaries, elders, and the believing communities and their representatives, respectively.

Conclusions from the Bible

In the first chapter we already went thoroughly into the meaning of thought in the Bible. God desires that we think when we study the Bible and to do the same when we apply his word. Even in cases where the Bible does not give concrete guidelines, we should come to good solutions by reflecting on things. It is therefore in no way astonishing that in the Bible itself the Bible is interpreted with common sense. In opposition to an exaggerated pharisaical view of the Sabbath, Jesus argues reasonably from everyday experience and from the Holy Scriptures. In doing this he draws upon texts and examples that have absolutely nothing directly to do with the topic.

An example of reasonable argumentation

> In Matthew 12:11-12 Jesus asks: "If any of you has a sheep and it falls into a pit on the Sabbath, will you not take hold of it and lift it out? How much more valuable is a man than a sheep! Therefore it is lawful to do good on the Sabbath" (similar argumentation for an ox in Luke 14:5). In Luke 13:15 Jesus refers to the accepted and allowed watering of oxen and donkeys on the Sabbath, where he has to address the accusation that on the Sabbath no crippled person was allowed to be healed.

An example of reasonable conclusions

> In Matthew 12:5 Jesus asks: "Or haven't you read in the Law that on the Sabbath the priests in the temple desecrate the day and yet are innocent?" In Mark 2:23-28 (corresponding to Matthew 12:1-7; Luke 6:1-5) Jesus justifies picking some heads of grain (Mark 2: 23b) with a reference to the fact that David, when he was starving, was allowed to eat the consecrated bread in the temple (Mark 2: 25-26; 1 Samuel 21:4-7). What Jesus does is to transfer to the Sabbath a situation that in detail is completely different and has nothing to do with the Sabbath. In John 7:23 Jesus says: "Now if a child can be circumcised on the Sabbath so that the law of Moses may not be broken, why are you angry with me for healing the whole man on the Sabbath?" The

completely natural command to care for the individual's survival, as well as the command in the Holy Scriptures to circumcise a child on a particular day, was more important than holding to the Sabbath command.

Examples of ethical guidelines which in the Bible do not have to do with references to God's word but are rather based on reasonable considerations or conclusions:
- 1 Corinthians 5: 9-10: "I have written you in my letter not to associate with sexually immoral people – not at all meaning the people of this world who are immoral, or the greedy and swindlers, or idolaters. In that case you would have to leave this world."
- Romans 3: 5-6: "But if our unrighteousness brings out God's righteousness more clearly, what shall we say? That God is unjust in bringing his wrath on us? (I am using a human argument.) Certainly not! If that were so, how could God judge the world?"
- Proverbs 22:25: (against associating with those people easily angered) "… or you may learn his ways and get yourself ensnared."
- Proverbs 22:27: (against pledging security for debts) "… if you lack the means to pay, your very bed will be snatched from under you."
- Proverbs 23:21: (against gluttony) "… for drunkards and gluttons become poor, and drowsiness clothes them in rags."
- Proverbs 25:8: "… do not bring hastily to court, for what will you do in the end if your neighbor puts you to shame?"
- Proverbs 27:24: "… for riches do not endure forever, and a crown is not secure for all generations."

These examples illustrate that norms, commands and regulations are not there to be parroted but rather to be thought about and applied. Biblical norms in no way stand in opposition to other sources for ethics, but rather they are complemented by them. God has so desired this and has made mankind in this manner.

2.2. Normative leadership means applying and interpreting

Diverse types of commands

The Bible is not presented to us as a collection of various basic regulations and values, which one can quickly learn and then immediately call upon in whatever situation one finds oneself. God's commands and ordinances are, rather, announced in the context of large literary diversity and in a range of manners of expression.[80] We find, for example, completely general, universally valid, and positively formulated commands (e.g., "You should love ...") as well as completely general, universally valid, negatively formulated commands (e.g., "You shall not covet ..."). Prohibitions protect a value and they renounce things that have no merit. To serve God and uphold his value ordinances means necessarily to not serve idols and those things which have no merit.

There are case studies which can serve for similar situations, and there are commands that declare the priority of obligations (e.g., Hosea 6:6; Matthew 9:13; 12:7) or that request to first do this and then that (comp. 1 Samuel 15:22; Ps 51:17, 19, 21; Jeremiah 7:22-23). Many commands only give instructions for a situation where other commands have already been violated (e.g., texts regarding divorce). Other commands define clear exceptions (e.g., killing in self-defense). Others, in turn, mention no exceptions, although exceptions are known from other texts or are presupposed as self-evident.

There are things which the Holy Scriptures expressly endorse but never raises to the point of a command. Fasting is a good example of this. While great blessing rests upon fasting, and we find many biblical models for it, fasting is neither presented as a duty for particular people or situations or as a general duty.[81]

Besides the directly valid commands and those which can immediately be put into practice, there is wisdom. Wisdom makes the correct decision dependent on the respective situation and can only act correctly if the involved parties are known. Wisdom can be passed on in the form of proverbs, parables, archetypal narratives, and object lessons. They contain life experiences which are only applicable as a rule (e.g., Proverbs 15:1; 22:6) but are not compulsory. We will address the issue of wisdom at greater length later.

The five levels of law

The Bible does not impart ethics in a unilinear fashion, solely in the form of established commands alone. Rather, it does this along the entire spectrum between basic statements, on the one hand, and actual case examples, on the other hand. In this way one can, for instance, differentiate between

---

[80] Comp. the overview by Walter C. Kaiser. Towards Old Testament Ethics. Zondervan: Grand Rapids (MI), 1983. pp. 64-66.

[81] Comp. R. T. Foster. "Fasting." pp. 376-378 in: David J. Atkinson, David H. Field (ed.). New Dictionary of Christian Ethics and Pastoral Theology. IVP: Downers Grove (IL), 1995.

five levels of Old Testament law: 1) basic concerns; 2) basic commandments; 3) rules for implementation; 4) case studies using individuals; and 5) case studies using animals.

Of course, other levels could also be delineated. And it is natural that one does not find every level represented for each topic. The point is not the number; rather, the point is the nature of law and commands as they range between entirely general statements and completely concrete examples.

Two or more levels are often addressed together in one verse, as we already saw in 1 Timothy 5:16-17. Most of the time the same principle is generally formulated as well as exemplified through the use of a case example. This can be seen, for example, in Proverbs 15:16-17: "Better a little with the fear of the Lord than great wealth with turmoil. Better a meal of vegetables where there is love than a fattened calf with hatred" (also comp. Proverbs 16:8; 17:1).

The five levels of law

Example 1: Wages

- 1st level: God's legal requirement
- 2nd level: Everyone receives a wage for what he does
- 3rd level: Everyone should receive a wage for his work
- 4th level: Application to elders
- 5th level: Case example with oxen

Detailed justification for example 1:

- 1st level: Romans 1:32, "God's righteous decree"
- 2nd level: 1 Corinthians 3:8, "… each will be rewarded according to his own labor;" 4th level, 5th level, and 3rd level (in this order): 1 Timothy 5:17-18: (4): "The elders who direct the affairs of the church well are worthy of double honor, especially those whose work is preaching and teaching. For the Scripture says' [5th], 'Do not muzzle the ox while it is treading out the grain,' and [3rd] 'The worker deserves his wages'" (from Deuteronomy 25:4 and quoted in 1 Corinthians 9:9 and in Luke 10:7).[82] Whatever applies to oxen is of course applicable for all animals, and it is all the more applicable to people.

---

[82] This quotes the Old and New Testaments simultaneously and speaks for an early estimation of the composition of the Gospel of Luke (comp. Heinz Warnecke, Thomas Schirrmacher. War Paulus wirklich auf Malta? Hänssler: Neuhausen, 1992. p. 227).

2. Normative decisions

Example 2: murder
- 1st level: Brotherly love
- 2nd level: Do not murder
- 3rd level: Manslaughter at the time of burglary
- 4th level: Case example of a fence on the roof
- 5th level: Case example of cisterns

Detailed justification for example 2:
- 1st level: Leviticus 19:18: "… but love your neighbor as yourself."
- 2nd level: Exodus 20:13: "You shall not murder."
- 3rd level: Exodus 22:1-2: "If a thief is caught breaking in and is struck so that he dies, the defender is not guilty of bloodshed; but if it happens after sunrise, he is guilty of bloodshed."
- 4th level: Deuteronomy 22:8: "When you build a new house, make a parapet around your roof so that you may not bring the guilt of bloodshed on your house if someone falls from the roof." This command also naturally applies to parallel cases: It is also manslaughter if one does not think about others and allows others to endanger themselves.
- 5th level: Leviticus 21:33-34: "If a man uncovers a pit [or a well] or digs one [or lets it be opened] and fails to cover it and an ox or a donkey falls into it, the owner of the pit must pay for the loss …" Again, this is an example of case law where the example has to do with animals, yet it applies all the more to people. Jesus also argued about the Sabbath with laws relating to animals. He did this to justify people's actions (e.g., Luke 13:15-17; 14:4-6; Matthew 12:10-12).

Case law and ethic of principles

Regarding the law about providing a parapet on a flat roof, Luther wrote the following: "This can be a proverbial and general law, that in public community things are so built, and one behaves in such a manner, that one does not cause others to be exposed to any dangers, disadvantages or damages …"[83]

---

[83] Martin Luther. "Anmerkungen zum fünften Buch Mosis." cols. 1370-1639 in: Martin Luther. Sämtliche Schriften. ed. Johann Georg Walch. Vol. 3. Verlag der Lutherischen Buchhandlung: Groß Oesingen, 1986 (1910² reprint), here col. 1565 (sic). In Old and New Testament times houses had flat roofs that were also used. Grass grew on the roof (Isaiah 37:27; Psalm 129:6), that animals were sometimes allowed to eat. Women spread things out on the roof so that they would dry (Joshua 2:6) and in the summer tents were put up on the roof and people slept there (2 Samuel 16:22; comp. Nehemiah 8:16; 1 Samuel 9:25). A person was safe on the

Since case law applies to similar situations and illustrates the causative principle – even in the case of manslaughter – this command also applies in cultures that have other types of roofs. It also applies to other life situations in which it is possible to take other preventative measures for people. That a parapet should be a protection on a flat roof, and that a pit should have a protection around it, means that every person is responsible for injuries and death in the case where he does not protect or warn others who are unknowing. In all legislation that is influenced by Christianity, there are corresponding provisions such as, for instance, that areas around road construction sites and pits and manholes be clearly sealed off.

A case law (casuistry, from the Latin *casus*, the case) is a law that illustrates a general principle by using a definite example.[84] Martin Honecker quite rightly writes: "Casuistry is the 'explanation of individual cases' in morals and jurisprudence. The word is largely used as a negative label when it is understood as a synonym for 'hairsplitting' and 'sophistry,' but casuistry first of all means – and this as a matter of fact is quite well justified – to apply rules to an individual case ..."[85]

Example from the state sector

> Even German jurisprudence, which perhaps more than in any other country tries to formulate innumerable foundational laws without individual case examples, does not work when from the case examples explicit legal principles cannot be derived for making decisions at a later time.
>
> In countries such as Great Britain,[86] in which the written law does not play as great a role as in Germany, legal decisions are to a much greater extent made on the basis of case law and precedent decisions. It is by all means doubtful whether one could produce a body of law that gets along without case law. "No legal system can completely dispense with casuistry."[87]

---

roof (Matthew 24:17). Important news was called out from roofs (Isaiah 15:3; Jeremiah 48:38; Matthew 10:27), which led to people subsequently meeting on roofs (Isaiah 22:1). When people gathered in a house, the roof could be uncovered and people could get to the center of the house as the friends of the paralytic were able to do in Mark 2:4; Luke 5:19 in order to bring him to Jesus.

[84] Comp. P. D. Toon. "Casuistry." pp. 52-53 in: R. K. Harrison (ed.). Encyclopedia of Biblical and Christian Ethics. Thomas Nelson: Nashville (TN), 1987.

[85] Martin Honecker. Einführung in die Theologische Ethik. Walter de Gruyter: Berlin, 1990. p. 170; comp. on casuistry p. 170-175.

[86] Ibid. p. 171 the following is written: "English law has remained case-oriented, casuistic until this day."

[87] Ibid. p. 170; comp. also Axel Denecke. Wahrhaftigkeit: Eine evangelische Kasuistik. Vandenhoeck & Ruprecht, Göttingen, 1971, even if Denecke goes in a completely different direction in details.

2. Normative decisions

Biblical case laws are of course not case laws in the sense of such precedent decisions. They are, as are basic commands, enacted once and for all; the canon of these case laws does not expand. Biblical case laws are commands that illustrate foundational principles on the basis of a particular case, and they can and must be transferrable to similar cases.

Examples for case law

The command that a millstone should not be given as security (Deuteronomy 24:6) naturally does not mean that only millstones may not be given as security. Rather, it refers to everything that is required for survival. It is also the case in German law that what serves for survival in daily life may not be given as security, even if the things included in the list today appear exaggerated (e.g., a television set).

The commands regarding blind and deaf people, "Cursed is the man who leads the blind astray on the road" (Deuteronomy 27:18) and "Do not curse the deaf or put a stumbling block in front of the blind, but fear your God," refer not only to the examples named but convey the idea that people are not to take advantage of others' disabilities. Rather, one is to be considerate of these people. Job was for this reason "eyes to the blind and feet to the lame" and "a father to the needy" (Job 29:15-16). These provisions have strongly shaped our culture.

In the Old Testament petty larceny of food is not theft: "If you enter your neighbor's vineyard, you may eat all the grapes you want, but do not put any in your basket. If you enter your neighbor's grain field, you may pick kernels with your hands, but you must not put a sickle to his standing grain" (Deuteronomy 23:24-25). This is a typical case law that of course does not just apply to grapes and grains. Rather, it sets down that the amount needed to meet one's needs is exempt from punishment.

Case law points to the fact that biblical ethics are an ethic of principles. It is decisive that for each command, out of which external visible application arises, a basic divine principle is first recognized. The highest principle is love towards God and neighbor. It lies at the bottom of all commands, and they can only be understood from that standpoint. Additional principles are derived there from,, which form the basis for concrete case laws.

An ethic of principle is of great importance for applying Old Testament commands in New Testament times, since it is often the case that in the New Testament a command's Old Testament principle is particularly emphasized. An ethic of principles is also of importance for the application of biblical commands in the present and in the ever new cultural situations of the world. What is decisive is how the basic principle is put into practice. Old Testament law, for example, requires "righteousness in the gates."

This is due to the fact that the Israelites' court system took place "in the gates." What is decisive is the principle of righteousness. Perhaps what is also decisive is the public character of holding court and not, however, the city gate as such, which many cultures do not have.

If one is speaking of casuistry, one has to differentiate the Old Testament from later Jewish casuistry. Old Testament casuistry illustrates a basic command with specific cases and examples, whereby the principle expressed therein should then be applied to similar cases. For this reason the cases discussed represent only a portion of the imaginable cases. *Casuistry alone is too concrete to derive truly basic principles from it, but to do without casuistry leaves ethics and law too abstract and distanced from reality.*

Furthermore, inner-biblical casuistry, which can call upon the authority of God's word, has to be distinguished from interpreters' casuistry, which tries to apply biblical ordinances to present day cases. The latter is acceptable, but the conclusions drawn from it cannot be placed in the same category as a command of God, such as is the case, for instance, in the Talmud in Judaism or in Catholicism's canon law.

Example from family life

> The guideline relating to sleep is that every person needs adequate sleep. This basic principle means something else for a baby than it means for a retired grandparent. At first, parents simply place their small children in bed. Later they set a time for the children to go to bed. The general principle regarding sleep is not something one would use with a nine year old child. A teenager receives more general instruction and has to go to bed on his own. At that point the child should understand the reasons. When the child at some point leaves home, he carries the sole responsibility for himself and his health. Still, it might be sensible for him, for instance, to read a book about sleeping and find out what type of sleeper he is. When he marries, he has to coordinate his sleeping behavior with that of another person. And when children arrive, new changes are in the offing. What one sees is that the principle remains the same, while the application, on the on the other hand, can differ widely. Concrete stipulations help a child, and case examples help adults.

Example from the business sector

> It is good when a company's guidelines set down general values and goals, e.g., "Honesty with all customers." But this good and noble guideline does not become visible until it is illustrated with a concrete example. For this the company either has to issue some rules for implementation (e.g., when there is a complaint, the customer can take a look at the correspondence) or teach

2. Normative decisions

what that would mean in a concrete situation. For instance, a seminar could be held in which various situations are run through. In this manner specific examples are "practiced in advance." Neither the noble guideline nor the particular rule for implementation in a specific situation can alone express the concern of the company. Only the entire spectrum – from the general objective to application in a specific situation – allows one to recognize whether a company has nothing to hide and knows how to enhance an already good reputation.

Values are "only" a framework

"All human thought and action hang together with a worldview. Everyone arrays themselves and their actions within the framework of a comprehensive interpretation of man and the world, within which behavior first achieves meaning."[88]

The expression "framework" is fittingly used here. This is due to the fact that, as important as absolute values are, an individual cannot only live with them and make decisions solely on the basis of them. God's word sets a framework for our life, thought, and planning, but it does not fill out this framework. God does not live our life. Rather, he produces the conditions for it. Essential principles are often illustrated for us in the Holy Scriptures via case examples. But otherwise the Bible summons us to weigh things, think through them, consider, seek counsel, and then take responsibility for our decisions.

That is the reason why large portions of the Old Testament law are formulated negatively. ("You shall not ..."). The precise thing that disturbs many people is what has so much to do with freedom. The "not" sets boundaries without prescribing details. Gustav Friedrich Oehler observes the following with respect to Old Testament law: "The stipulations of the law are mainly found in detail in negative terms. The requirements go into detail regarding what an Israelite is not allowed to do ... However, it is easy to recognize that in respect to positive duties, the law in many cases only expresses things generally. The intention is not to expressly mandate, but rather to put forth facts, examples, and institutions which allow the positive aspects to freely flourish."[89]

Job acknowledges (23:12): "I have not departed from the commands of his lips; I have treasured the words of his mouth more than my daily

---

[88] Hansjörg Hemminger. Psychotherapie: Weg zum Glück? Zur Orientierung auf dem Psychomarkt. Münchener Reihe. Evangelischer Presseverband für Bayern: München, 1987. p. 5.

[89] Gustav Friedrich Oehler. Theologie des Alten Testaments. J. F. Steinkopf: Stuttgart, 1891.³ p. 289 (sic).

bread." Job's love for the poor, who are described in this connection, goes well beyond that which is required. Still, on the basis of this fact, one may not come to the opposite conclusion that love can get along without order and confines.

Since one's view of values, as well as one's view of the Bible as a framework, are together central for the question of how Christian leaders decide, we want to take a look at several additional examples.

Example from the state sector

> The Bible speaks clearly about the significance of marriage and warns us about crossing the boundaries that would ultimately destroy a marriage. But the Bible is also not a handbook for everyday married life. When it comes to how this most important human relationship is explicitly fashioned, the Bible is silent. It talks about love, about being there for each other, and about the joys of sexuality. Boundaries are also set, but the marriage partners have to pay attention to all the small everyday things themselves. What God, as the creator of marriage, thinks about marriage is infinitely important as a framework for marriage and for providing the stamp of authorization, but it does not replace shaping a marriage in the here and now. My wife would not take it as a sign of a good marriage if every morning I would read the biblical commands relating to marriage and yet she had to remind me that my loveless behavior did not square with them. Reading and quoting Bible verses does not produce love. I have to rack my brains about what is best for my wife and how I can express my love to her in new ways. The biblical ordinances for marriage are good and necessary, but they can only protect the essence, not produce it. Love does not act against the command, but love is not equivalent with not breaking the command. Rather, it is something much greater. People who only speak about the ordinances might be good architects who know everything about building houses and can win every case against the authorities and construction companies. But they might have no interest in what is essentially at issue – the people who live in the house. Without people, every house, regardless of how good it might be, is of no consequence.

Example from the state and family sectors

> It is crucial for understanding biblical commands to see that they present a type of constitution. And just as in a modern constitutional state under the rule of law, already in the Old Testament state it was the law, not the individual, that has the highest authority. (Today one can bring legal action against the German Chancellor; in contrast, one could not bring legal action against the German Emperor.) Similarly, God's law is a type of constitution for the family. It is not the parents who are the law for the children. Rather, both the parents and the children are subordinate to the same law, to the

same creation ordinances God has decreed. Parental authority is derived from this divine constitution, which provides rights and calls for duties on the parts of parents and children. This is tangibly expressed by the fact that parents are themselves measured by these ordinances and must apologize for breaking them. If parents lie to their children, they have to admit it, just as their children do, and apologize. Anything else would have devastating results. I know many children of Christian parents where especially the father has never apologized. He is always right, even when he was wrong. What a disastrous educational message! And what sort of message does this send about the values that one is constantly mentioning: they apparently only apply if a person has to obey. If a person later becomes "the commander," he gets to defy them!

Example from church life

Imagine a church wishes to call a pastor. It is natural that a number of particular points will play a role, This could include, for instance, the fact that the candidate agree with the church's confession of faith, its lifestyle or moral conduct. Still, there are numerous additional factors within this framework which will also influence the decision and which have little or nothing to do with the confession of faith. An example is the question of whether the pastor's children can find an appropriate school in the location. A further good example has to do with the pastor's talents. That these things play a significant role in the question of a call is predicted by the Bible. Still, how can an individual find out which talents or gifts he has and which talents are required in the particular location in question? It is only via an interplay between the situation, family background, experience, tradition, and personal attitude that a correct decision can be made.

Example from the state sector

Imagine that the state requires a basic ethical foundation that, among others, contains provisions to the effect that one of the primary duties is to protect human life. Given this existing foundation of basic values, the state will, for example, derive its set of traffic regulations to a large degree upon such a foundation. For instance, this could have to do with maximum speeds, and for this an individual does not require knowledge of the Bible or of Christian textbooks. Traffic regulations are for this reason, on the one hand, anchored in the basic values of people (see §1 of the German traffic code, for example). At the same time, in their explicit application the regulations are tied to innumerable technical and ever changing details. Traffic regulations are ineffectual if they are not anchored in some basic value structure. They are similarly ineffectual if they are not continually asking how these values are here and now best suited to protect people.

Example from the business sector

Honesty and reliability are indispensable foundations for all business dealings, whether these dealings have to do with trading goods within a pygmy tribe or trading on electronic securities exchanges around the world. Every economy can only tolerate a certain amount of dishonesty and deceit. This is demonstrated with every purchase. When I pay at the register, there arises a moment of indispensible trust, because goods and money cannot be completely simultaneously exchanged. If I receive the goods first, I could maintain, "I have already paid." If, however, I have to pay first, the cashier could maintain, "You have not paid yet." The less trust that reigns, the more complicated the transaction becomes. In the end the transaction can become as complicated as a hostage exchange in a film about the Wild West or the taking of a hostage where mistrust dominates. And still, the necessary trust in others to which I refer is only a framework. Honesty and reliability alone do not produce an economy. Yet everything that happens within this framework has to be developed and in the process is extremely multifaceted.

A further example

When the Old Testament calls for uniformity and reliability insofar as weights and measures for business are concerned, the values involved are not simply private values. Rather, the values form the basis for every functioning economy and are the precondition for equitable prosperity. Two values are at work that are referred to in the Ten Commandments but which are also basically recognized in every secular society. These values are, namely, honesty over against lying ("You shall not give false testimony") and the right to property ownership over against theft ("You shall not steal") as well as the internal attitude ("You shall not covet"). Whoever deceitfully infringes upon these values destroys not only personal relationships but puts a strain on and even can destroy the entire society. In Amos 8:4-6 God warns about oppressing the poor and the weak by using dishonest weights and measures. Question 110 of the 1563 Heidelberg Catechism deliberately refers to the Old Testament standards of honest weights and measures in its explanation of the commandment against stealing. It also binds the state to monitor this and indeed shows just how comprehensively the Reformation viewed the Old Testament commandment against theft: "What does God forbid in the eighth commandment? He forbids not only outright theft and robbery, punishable by law. But in God's sight theft also includes cheating and swindling our neighbor by schemes made to appear legitimate, such as: inaccurate measurements of weight, size, or volume; fraudulent merchandising; counterfeit money; excessive interest; or any other means forbidden by God. In addition he forbids all greed and pointless squandering of his gifts."[90] Although values set in the Bible are unambiguous, the Bible does not speak about measurements, weights, and currency units that are valid for all times and cultures. How could that be possible, anyway? Measurements, weights and currencies are subject to continual change. Yet the principle of reliability of the data a seller reveals is at all times of foundational importance for the economy. Admittedly, explicit implementation has to be repeatedly adjusted.

Honest measures, weights, and scales

Commands
- Proverbs 16:11 – "Honest scales and balances are from the Lord; all the weights in the bag are of his making."
- Proverbs 20:10, 23 – "Differing weights and differing measures – the Lord detests them both… The Lord detests differing weights, and dishonest scales do not please him."
- Leviticus 19:35-36 – "Do not use dishonest standards when measuring length, weight or quantity. Use honest scales and honest weights, an honest ephah and an honest hin."[91]
- Deuteronomy: 25:13-16 – "Do not have two differing weights in your bag – one heavy, one light. Do not have two differing measures in your house – one large, one small. You must have accurate and honest weights and measures, so that you may live long in the land the Lord your God is giving you. For the Lord your God detests anyone who does these things, anyone who deals dishonestly.
- Ezekiel 45:9-12 – "… do what is just and right … You are to use accurate scales, an accurate ephah and an accurate bath. The ephah and the bath are to be the same size, the bath containing a tenth of a homer and the ephah a tenth of a homer; the homer is to be the standard measure for both. The shekel is to consist of twenty gerahs. Twenty shekels plus twenty-five shekels plus fifteen shekels equal one mina."[92]

Criticism made on the basis of these commands
- Hosea 12:7 – "The merchant uses dishonest scales; he loves to defraud."
- Amos 8:4-5 – "Hear this, you who trample the needy and do away with the poor of the land … that we may sell grain … skimping the measure, boosting the price and cheating with dishonest scales …"

---

[90] Quoted from http://www.crcna.org/pages/heidelberg_commandments.cfm#QandA%20110
[91] These are Hebrew measures.
[92] The terms are various Hebrew designations of measure.

- Micah 6:10-11 – "Am I still to forget, O wicked house, your ill-gotten treasures and the short ephah, which is accursed? Shall I acquit a man with dishonest scales, with a bag of false weights?

Example from the business sector

The famous saying "the worker deserves his wages" (1 Corinthians 9:9; Luke 10:7; comp. Deuteronomy 25:4) makes every type of work valuable and creates an obligation for equitable pay that may not be withheld (Mark 10:19; Deuteronomy 24:14; Leviticus 19:13; James 5:4). The command is understood in the New Testament equally as an obligation of the church towards elders (1 Timothy 5:17-18) as well as a basic criticism of business people and of materialism: "Look! The wages you failed to pay the workmen who mowed your fields are crying out against you. The cries of the harvesters have reached the ears of the Lord Almighty" (James 5:4). Not to pay wages or not to pay them completely or too late is grievous theft: "Do not steal ... Do not deceive one another ... Do not defraud your neighbor or rob him. Do not hold back the wages of a hired man overnight" (Leviticus 9:11-13). The Old Testament generally warns rather often about oppressing others by paying low wages and uses in this clear formulations that even Karl Marx could not outdo: "Do not defraud your neighbor or rob him" (Leviticus 19:13). "Do not take advantage of a hired man who is poor and needy, whether he is a brother Israelite or an alien living in one of your towns [within your jurisdiction]. Pay him his wages each day before sunset, because he is poor and is counting on it. Otherwise he may cry to the Lord against you, and you will be guilty of sin" (Deuteronomy 24: 14-15). "Woe to him who builds his palace by unrighteousness, his upper rooms by injustice, making his countrymen work for nothing, not paying them for their labor" (Jeremiah 22:13). The biblical statements about the binding nature of agreements relating to labor offered and their compensation as well as the necessity and entitlement to payment are of wide ranging importance. Still, they are not so formulated that we concretely know exactly how a labor agreement is supposed to look and which wage is appropriate. God alludes to the necessity of the legal certainty of a labor agreement and to adequate compensation. However, the concrete configuration reached between the contractual parties as well as the institutions in charge of overseeing the legal aspects are items that are entrusted to others and may change in times and cultures.

How can this be conveyed to a secular environment?
All human activity occurs and is ordered within the framework of a comprehensive interpretation of man and the world. It is within such a structure that everything we do finds its meaning. We need both: immovable boundaries and the flexibility of real life for new situations. Values are indispen-

sable. They set borders that people step over to their own detriment. However, these boundaries and knowledge about values are not enough to produce them. The dignity of man, according to our constitution, is inviolable. That is an essential foundation of our society and of our system of jurisprudence. This basis, however, cannot bring about a situation where we actually deal with each other in a way that we truly esteem each other. Likewise, this basis does not say how the value 'human dignity' is expressed in everyday life. What does 'human dignity' mean in interaction with a baby, with an employee, and with the former German Chancellor? What does 'human dignity' mean in the workplace, on the tennis court, and in war? And how do we deal with people who trample the dignity of others under foot? Without a 'constitution' no human society can survive, whether it be large or small. However, a constitution cannot replace real life, but only order and protect it in general.

Helping to translate

One of the main tasks of the church is to help its members translate the Bible's teachings into their respective areas of life by concrete example. This happens far too rarely, and there are numerous reasons for this. Our purely theoretical training for full time workers, far removed from practical experience, is as faulty as is the idea that teachings for people should be concentrated on 52 sermons per year. The exclusion of certain areas of life (e.g., the idea that 'Jesus' church has nothing to do with business and politics') is also faulty.

The best example of how education and vocational training are unified towards promoting independence under one principle is the training of the twelve Apostles. A pedagogical program lay at the basis of their training, in which course Jesus taught his followers over three years and found himself in one-on-one conversations as well as in group discussions. In any case, what was involved in the training of Jesus' followers included teaching and life questions, everyday life and lectures, special instructions and individual counseling, and work in public along with discussions outside public view. This was all intertwined in a way that provided integrated training. At the commencement of their program of training one reads: "Jesus went up on a mountainside and called to him those he wanted, and they came to him. He appointed twelve – designating them apostles – that they might be with him and that he might send them out to preach and to have authority to drive out demons" (Mark 3:13-16). On the one hand, Jesus limited himself to a small number of followers, "that they might be with him," just as a father would only tend to only a small number of children. The twelve Apostles were supposed to share their lives with Jesus.

No one can simultaneously share his life with many people. No one can fulfill his role as a parent if he has forty children. If someone has forty children to take care of, we are probably talking about an orphanage. Without placing the sacrificial work of educators into question, they can never replace the intensive child rearing that a father and mother can provide.

On the other hand, Jesus chose them so "that he might send them out." The intensive fellowship and their dependence on him had the goal of sending out independent and seasoned workers. The Disciples were not meant to live forever in close fellowship with Jesus, but rather carry on Jesus' mandate independently. In John 20:21 Jesus tells his followers: "As the Father has sent me, I am sending you" (comp. John 17:18). The goal of the close attachment to Jesus lies in the coming Great Commission: "Therefore go and make disciples of all nations ... teaching them to obey everything I have commanded you" (Matthew 18:18-20). The Disciples were to do everything that Jesus had demonstratively taught them. However, this was not to take place under his continual supervision and presence in person but rather in a convinced, independent, and unmistakable manner.

Example from family life

> The rearing of a child should lead from the extremely close symbiotic community that is the case when one is a small child, to the gradual independence of that same child who later, as a youth, becomes part of a community that is continually changing and who in turn also changes the community. Grown-up children, then, do not owe their parents obedience. What remains are the values that were communicated to them by parents, teachers, and other people with whom they had relationships. What my parents enjoyed does not have to appeal to me any longer. I have my own tastes and basically there is nothing that goes against following that appetite. With my own family I have developed a new cuisine. And what do I have to thank my parents for with respect to eating? It is the values having to do with eating. There is a thankfulness toward God that is, for instance, expressed in saying grace at a meal. (By the way, this looks completely different to the way my parents do it, and my children will in turn do it differently.) God is more important than the food. For me, the topic of 'food' means service to people who do not have enough to eat, and this is expressed by my involvement in the leadership of an international relief organization for the Third World. My parents never did that concretely. And still, it has to do with their values that brought about fruit in me. What is decisive is not that the children adopt the lifestyle of their parents, but rather that the basic values God gave humanity are recognized and applied independently.

We have to learn anew to translate basic values and arrangements into concrete situations in our life. The best place for this is the family and church. Whoever has not learned the necessary abilities there should try and get them from whoever can help. Whoever is not in a position to change a five-hundred Euro bill into small change cannot, regardless of how much wealth he has, buy an ice cream.

2.3. Normative leadership means understanding mandates

The four mandates

We want to take up the teaching of the four mandates as referred to by Dietrich Bonhoeffer. This teaching assumes that God has created different relationships and communities which have different mandates, and for that reason they have to be governed differently. According to this teaching, there are four independent federations or institutions: marriage (family), work, the authorities, and the church.

Ray R. Sutton writes in this connection: "God uses the word covenant to describe all relationships in the Scriptures. His relationship to himself, to his creation as well as the relationships within the creation: family, work, church, and the state."[93]

A covenant comes about by an oath (pledge) before God and is subject to a covenant law, the main features of which are derived from the creation ordinances. There is no 'natural' authority, only authority that is given by God and authorities that are entrusted by him with limited mandates.

In this way one arrives at the number four. Which institutions has God directly set up and with which covenantal structure (oath and constitution)? For work, marriage, the state, and the church this can be demonstrated, but not for a fifth. The school, for instance is derived from the authority of child rearing in the four covenantal institutions, but itself is no institution directly given by God.

Dietrich Bonhoeffer[94] called these covenants "mandates" and wrote, "The Bible knows of four such mandates: work, marriage, the state, the

---

[93] Ray R. Sutton. "A Tract on Covenant." Covenant Renewal 3 (1989) 9: 1-4, here p. 1.

[94] Comp. with Bonhoeffer's teaching on mandates by Rainer Mayer. "Die Bedeutung von Bonhoeffers Mandatenlehre für eine moderne politische Ethik." pp. 58-80 in: Rainer Mayer, Peter Zimmerling (ed.). Dietrich Bonhoeffer heute: Die Aktualität seines Lebens und Werkes. Brunnen: Gießen, 1992; Rainer Mayer. "Zuviel Staat oder zuwenig Staat?" pp. 126-158 in: Rainer Mayer, Peter Zimmerling. Dietrich

church."⁹⁵ According to Bonhoeffer, one cannot separate these mandates into worldly and divine. Indeed, due to the fact that these mandates have been given by God means that any retreat from the worldly into a purely spiritual realm is impossible.⁹⁶ For Bonhoeffer all these mandates have their origin in heaven.⁹⁷ Marriage has its archetype in Christ and the church. The family has its archetype in God as Father with the Son. Work has its archetype in creation and service to God. And finally, the state has its archetype in the lordship of Christ.

Bonhoeffer's teaching of the mandates was without doubt motivated by Luther's teaching of three stations (see below)⁹⁸ but it uses the concept 'mandate' "in order to avoid rigid thinking with regard to regulations and thinking in spatial terms."⁹⁹ The switch in wording, however, changes nothing regarding the fact that Bonhoeffer is counted among classical ethicists of order.¹⁰⁰

The Reformed theologian (and for a time Prime Minister of the Netherlands) Abraham Kuyper also referred to three 'systems of order' next to the

---

Bonhoeffer: Beten und Tun des Gerechten: Glaube und Verantwortung im Widerstand. Brunnen: Gießen, 1997. pp. 143-146; Rainer Mayer. Christuswirklichkeit: Grundlagen, Entwicklung und Konsequenzen der Theologie Dietrich Bonhoeffers. Arbeiten zur Theologie II, 15. Calwer Verlag: Stuttgart, 1980² (1969¹). pp. 179-186; Jürgen Weißbach. Christologie und Ethik bei Dietreich Bonhoeffer. Theologische Existenz heute NF 131. Chr. Kaiser: München, 1966. pp. 37-45; Jürgen Moltmann. Herrschaft Christi und soziale Wirklichkeit nach Dietrich Bonhoeffer. Theologische Existenz heute NF 71. Chr. Kaiser: München, 1959. pp. 45-61 (Moltmann fundamentally changed his mind later); Reinhard Hauber. "Das Mandat der Ehe bei Dietrich Bonhoeffer." pp. 89-104 in: Wilfried Veeser, et al. (ed.). Theologische Auseinandersetzung mit dem Denken unserer Zeit. Vol. 3. Hänssler: Neuhausen, 1984.

⁹⁵ Dietrich Bonhoeffer. Ethik. Chr. Kaiser: München, 1949. p. 70; similarly also p. 216; comp. with the individual mandates pp. 70-74 and Dietrich Bonhoeffer. Dietrich Bonhoeffer Werke. Vol. 6: Ethik. Chr. Kaiser: München, 1992. pp. 392-398 (with comments).
⁹⁶ Dietrich Bonhoeffer. Ethik. op. cit., p. 70.
⁹⁷ Comp. Jürgen Moltmann. Herrschaft Christi und soziale Wirklichkeit nach Dietrich Bonhoeffer. op. cit., p. 54.
⁹⁸ So also Jürgen Moltmann. Herrschaft Christi und soziale Wirklichkeit nach Dietrich Bonhoeffer. op. cit., pp. 46-47.
⁹⁹ Ibid., p. 49.
¹⁰⁰ Comp. with Paul Althaus on ordinance ethics. Theologie der Ordnungen. 1935,² in part. pp. 13-16 (for creation ordinances), pp. 16-18 (section entitled "Die Ordnungen als Gesetz Gottes"). Ordinances "are at the same time given and ceded", and "at the same time a gift and a law of God," formulated accurately in this way by Althaus, ibid. p. 16.

2. Normative decisions

church, and they are directly subordinate to God: the family, the economy, and the state.[101]

John Witte summarizes the similar view held by the Dutch Calvinist philosopher Hermann Dooyeweerd in four points:[102] 1. All institutions have their genesis in creation. 2. God rules in an absolutely sovereign manner over all aspects of the creation, meaning that there is nothing in creation that is excluded from his authority. 3. "God's authority is a legal authority."[103] God rules thus via laws, natural laws, laws of logic, and via moral laws. 4. Every social institution has its own law and a legal duty within the framework of the creation (sphere sovereignty[104]). This leads to defending the "independent sovereignty of the church, the state, the family, and different economic organizations."[105]

Three of these covenants, family, church, and the state, are viewed by most confessions as basic, God-given institutions. To what extent work, that is to say the economy and the creation of culture, is subordinated to the family or is a separate, fourth covenant is variously seen. I am assuming the four covenants, but I will draw in arguments from those representatives of the three covenant view.

According to Luther there are "three types of rule in the world" that "God provides and maintains,"[106] namely the family, the state, and the church, and Luther sees them as having already been arranged in paradise.[107] "The three divine types of rule which the sophists call hierarchies are the rule of the home, worldly rule, and the rule of the church."[108]

---

[101] Comp. Alfred de Quervain. Die Heiligung. Ethik Erster Teil. Evangelischer Verlag: Zollikon, 1946.² p. 310-311.

[102] John Witte. "Introduction." pp. 11-30 in: Hermann Dooyeweerd. A Christian Theory of Social Institutions. The Hermann Dooyeweerd Foundation: La Jolla (CA); Paideia Press: St. Catharines (ON/CAN), 1986. pp. 16-17.

[103] Ibid. p. 16.

[104] Ibid. p. 17.

[105] Ibid.

[106] Quoted from Martin Luther. Sämtliche Schriften. ed. by Johann Georg Walch. Vol. 23. Verlag der Lutherischen Buchhandlung: Groß Oesingen, 1986 (Nachdruck von 1910²). Col. 1509 (also referenced there).

[107] Comp. to Luther's teaching on regiments by Wilhelm Maurer. Luthers Lehre von den drei Hierarchien und ihr mittelalterlicher Hintergrund. Bayerische Akademie der Wissenschaften, Philosophisch-Historische Klasse. Sitzungsberichte (1970) 4. Verlag der Bayerischen Akademie der Wissenschaften: München, 1970; Hans-Jürgen Prien. Luthers Wirtschaftsethik. Vandenhoeck & Ruprecht: Göttingen, 1992. pp. 162-170; Reinhard Schwarz. "Luthers Lehre von den drei Ständen und die drei Dimensionen der Ethik." Lutherjahrbuch: Organ der internationalen Lutherforschung 45 (1978) 15-34; Reinhard Schwarz. "Ecclesia; oeconomia; politia;

Luther also often calls the three types of rule, "foundations" or "orders,"[109] and with this he arguably, and in a polemical manner, wants to place something biblical where there had been other foundations and systems of orders.[110] For Luther, the hitherto existing foundations and systems of order had not been set down by God: "However, the holy systems of order and right foundations set down by God are three: the office of the priest, the station of marriage, and worldly authorities."[111]

Luther knew de facto not three but four types of rule. If one assembles the different "fathers" Luther refers to together, one find physical fathers, spiritual fathers, political fathers (*Landesvater*) and vocational fathers (lords, masters, etc.).[112] Luther writes in this connection:[113] "We have three

---

Sozialgeschichtliche und fundamentalethische Aspekte der protestantischen Drei-Stände-Theorie." pp. 78-88 in: Horst Renz, Friedrich Wilhelm Graf. Troeltsch-Studien 3: Protestantismus und Neuzeit. Gütersloher Verlagshaus Gerd Mohn: Gütersloh, 1984; Werner Elert. Morphologie des Luthertums. Zweiter Band: Sozialallehren und Sozialwirkungen des Luthertums. C. H. Beck: München, 1953². pp. 56-65; Peter Barth. Das Problem der natürlichen Theologie bei Calvin. Theologische Existenz heute 18. Chr. Kaiser: München, 1935. p. 57; F. Edward Cranz. An Essay on the Development of Luther's Thought on Justice, Law, and Society. Harvard Theological Studies 19. Harvard University Press: Cambridge (MA), 1959. pp. 160-161, 174-176; K. Köhler. "Die altprotestantische Lehre von den drei kirchlichen Ständen." Zeitschrift für Kirchenrecht 21/NF 6 (1886) 99-150, 193-231; Friedrich Lezius. "Gleichheit und Ungleichheit: Aphorismen zur Theologie und Staatsanschauung Luthers." pp. 285-326 in: Greifswalder Studien: Theologische Abhandlungen Hermann Cremer zum 25jährigen Professorenjubiläum dargebracht. C. Bertelsmann: Gütersloh, 1895; Karl-Heinz zur Mühlen. "Luther II. Theologie." 530-567 in: Gerhard Müller (ed.). Theologische Realenzyklopädie. Vol. 21. de Gruyter: Berlin, 2000/1991 (study edition), here pp. 557-560.

[108] Quoted from Martin Luther. Sämtliche Schriften. Vol. 23. op. cit., Col. 806 (also referenced there); comp. also "Each one of the three regiments, the spiritual, the worldly, and the regiment of the home, has its devil whereby it is hindered or corrupted," quoted from ibid. col. 1510 (also referenced there).

[109] Reinhard Schwarz. "Ecclesia; oeconomia; politia." op. cit., p. 83.

[110] According to Reinhard Schwarz. "Luthers Lehre von den drei Ständen und die drei Dimensionen der Ethik." op. cit., p. 17.

[111] Quoted from Martin Luther. Sämtliche Schriften. Vol. 23. op. cit. 1510 (sic).

[112] See Luther's exegesis of the Fourth Commandment (according to Reformed counting the Fifth Commandment) in his Large Catechism: Horst Georg Pöhlmann, et al. (ed.). Unser Glaube: Die Bekenntnisschriften der evangelisch-lutherischen Kirche. Ausgabe für die Gemeinde. GB Siebenstern 1289. Gütersloher Verlagshaus: Gütersloh, 1986. pp. 629-634, Sections 645-652; comp. Martin Honecker. Einführung in die Theologische Ethik. Walter de Gruyter: Berlin, 1990. pp. 294, 296.

[113] Later Lutheran theology also assumed a "directly installed schematic of the Kingdom of God," that is to say, three divine institutions or hierarchies, namely the

2. Normative decisions

types of fathers ...: the [fathers] according to blood, according to our house, and according to country."[114]

Different duties according to the four mandates

The four covenants and institutions or areas of life, respectively, have completely different duties and are directly subordinate to God. This is the case even if they are enmeshed with each other and their duties reach into other covenants.

Completely different penalties belong to the four covenants:
- In child rearing, the family punishes all the way up to closely defined corporal punishment
- Employers punish by reducing pay or by dismissal from work
- The church punishes by admonishment all the way up to church discipline
- The state punishes by fines and imprisonment all the way up to the maximum penalty ("Court ... be it death or banishment or fines or imprisonment" Ezra 7:26).

For this reason parents in the Old Testament did not have a right to sit in judgment over their children. Children, who in spite of punishment no longer wanted to obey their parents, were to be given over by their parents to the local court (Deuteronomy 21:18-21). The parental right does not go beyond a narrowly defined corporal punishment (Proverbs 19:18). Only the state may exercise force.

In every case, all four covenants or institutions, respectively, come into existence on a local level by choice and by an oath that follows, that is to say, a contract made by oath (constitution):
- In the family this occurs by the choice of a marriage partner, by engagement, and marriage (Malachi 2:14-16);
- In the church by the choice of overseers, elders, and deacons and their placement into service (ordination – Acts 14:23; comp. 6:1-6; 1:15-26);

State (in Latin *magistratus civilis*), the church (in Latin *status hierarchici*) and marriage and the family (in Latin status oeconomicus). It is by the designation of the latter as 'economic status' that a subordination of the economy to the family is made clear. I, however, place it next to the family (quotes from Carl Bernhard Hundeshagen. Calvinismus und staatsbürgerliche Freiheit; Hubert Languet. Wider die Tyrannen. hg. von Laure Wyss. Evangelischer Verlag: Zollikon, 1946. p. 18).

[114] Horst Georg Pöhlmann, et al. (ed.). Unser Glaube. op. cit., p. 634 (Section 652).

- In the work relationship by the choice of employer and employee and an employment contract (according to James 5:4 an employment contract is binding; comp. Matthew 20:1-16);
- In the state this occurs through the choice of representatives (comp. in the USA the House of Representatives; in the Old Testament this person is named an elder). The Old Testament 'parliament' of elders was called "the whole assembly of Israel" (1 Kings 12:3 and Joshua 12:2). The king was also "chosen" ("here is the king you have chosen," 1 Samuel 12:13[115]), because "a large population is a king's glory" (Proverbs 14:28). In addition, the king was installed by an oath made to the people and the parliament (2 Samuel 5:3-5; 2 Kings 11:4-12; 1 Kings 12:3-5, 12-17, 20).

By the way, all authorities had a right to receive compensation. Parents (1Timothy 5:17-18; Mark 7:7-13) receive payments when they are old. Elders receive compensation from the church (1Timothy 5:17-18; 1 Corinthians 9:9), and the state receives compensation via taxes. In the case of employers, payment occurs for the labor rendered by the employee or by the profit margin, respectively.

Different Aspects of the four mandates (by Karl Schock)

In the Old Testament, God describes all relationships between his creation, himself and also between different components of the creation with the word "covenant." A covenant (or a covenantal institution) comes into being by an oath before God and is subject to covenantal law (constitution). Every covenant is 'ruled' differently and in part follows differing ethical principles. Every person simultaneously belongs in each covenant, and all belong together. Covenants are not allowed to abusively dominate each other or mix with each other.

---

[115] The choice of a king is also meant in the royal law in Deuteronomy 17:14-20, when it is mentioned that the people should "... set a king over us ..." (Deuteronomy 17:15, 16).

2. Normative decisions

Aspect	Family/Person	Church	Work/Economy	State
Goals, methods of pursuing goals	Family membership, procreation, harmony	Justification, unity of belief	Revenues, success, efficiency, value creation, provision for life	Affluence, national unity, provision for life, social order, security
Goals achieved	Education, relationship building, care	Doctrines, church community life, sacraments	Training, self-actualization, legitimate pursuit of goals, egoism	Legislative, executive, military and police-based enforcement
Relationships involved	Blood relationships, love, physical and spiritual unity	'Body of Christ,' grace, love, spiritual unity, faith	A community of achievement and social orientation, obedience	National unity, language, culture
Authority, government	Biological father and mother	Spiritual father and mother	Employer, boss	Founding fathers, government
Manner of selection, contractual aspects	Choice of partner, engagement, marriage contract	Choice of bishops and leaders, ordination	Employment contract	Choice of representatives, oath of office
Compensation	Affection, acceptance	Justification, salvation, blessings	Wages, wealth	Recognition, titles, orders
Discipline	Child rearing, limited corporal punishment, divorce	Admonishment, church discipline	Minimum remuneration, incentives, dismissal	Property damages, imprisonment, police, military
Jurisdiction	Voluntariness	Dogma, church law	Corporate regulations and business charter	Governmental laws
Mediation	Fatherly and motherly authority	Teaching office, priestly and episcopal hierarchy	"The boss is always right," success structure, power of capitalism	Courts, authorities, state force
Laws	Love, acceptance, forgiveness and under certain circumstances divorce law	The principles of the kingdom of God, Sermon on the Mount	Market laws, competition, money ruling the world	Laws passed by the authorities to maintain order
Gratification	Security, children, relatives	Blessedness, being pleasing to God, spiritual health	Possessions, provisions for life, self-actualization	Homeland, culture, security
Dangers	Dependency, separation, deprivation of love	Indoctrination, excommunication	Loss of wealth, unemployment	Lack of freedom, military conflicts
Decision making; manner of forming the will	Agreement, family conferences	Church and community constitution, teaching office	Participative management, owner majority	Decision by democratic majority, constitution

The separation of church and state

On the basis of the existence of four 'covenants,' it is already apparent in the Old Testament that there is a separation of 'church' and 'state.' It is not by accident that the separation of church and state was introduced in the United States by convinced Christians. At the point where the state no longer knows that it is responsible to hold to God's creation ordinances, a battle of the state against Christianity begins out of what was a separation of church and state.

The separation of church and state was not introduced against Christianity. Rather, it was initiated and put into practice by Christians. In spite of the many aberrations in past centuries, there was no other religion where the separation of church and state was set up in this manner from the beginning as was the case with Christianity. While in other nations it was a matter of course that the ruler also had the function of the highest priest (or even as god), the Old as well as the New Testament had neither a king who was simultaneously the high priest nor a high priest who simultaneously determined the political direction.

The Old Testament differentiates itself from its environment, among others, in that it
- in the first place (according to the will of God) does not call for a king, thereby evidentially indicating that the state can also be ruled without a king exercising power,
- and in the second place the head of state, who even later was the king, was not the high priest. The king did not even have power of disposal over the priest and had to put up with the critique of the priests and prophets.

Clear examples of the separation in the Old Testament are the following:
- the difference between king and priest;
- the division of labor between Moses as law giver and Aaron as high priest;
- the division of labor between Nehemiah as governor and Ezra as priest;
- the division of labor between Deborah as prophet and Barak as judge and as a commander of armed forces;
- the double administration in Israel, as it was, for instance, expressed in 2 Chronicles 19:11: "Amariah the chief priest will be over you in any matter concerning the Lord, and Zebadiah son of Ishmael, the leader of the tribe of Judah, will be over you in any matter concerning the king." There were separate secular and spiritual jurisdictions (2 Chronicles 19:8);

2. Normative decisions

- the existence of two types of taxes, namely the tax for God (the "tithe") and the tax for the king ("tribute," "tax"). Jesus assumes this system of separation, although in the meantime the authorities had long since been a foreign power and not the king of Israel. "Give back to Caesar what is Caesar's, and to God what is God's" (Matthew 22:21; comp Proverbs 24:21; 1 Peter 2:17);
- the existence of two types of anointing (two types of anointing in 1 Chronicles 29:22: Solomon as "king" and Zadok as "priest");
- the existence of two central houses in Jerusalem ("House of the Lord" and "House of the king" in 2 Chronicles 7:11);
- the existence of two sets of statutes ("the law of your God" and the "law of the king" in Ezra 7:26).

The separation of "church" and "state" is expressed clearly in the words of Jesus: "Give back to Caesar what is Caesar's and to God what is God's" (Mark 12:17). Jesus simultaneously undertook to restrict the authority of the state, which at that time also wanted to rule and determine everything.

One of the composers of the Heidelberg Catechism, Zacharias Ursinus (1534-1583), wrote the following about the difference between the church and the state: "1. State force punishes *vi corporali* [equiv. to bodily force], the church only admonishes by the word and excludes from the congregation. 2. The state limits itself to the exercise of justice through punishment. The church, however, seeks the improvement and the salvation of the individual. 3. The state moves to punishment where the church offers brotherly admonishment, 'in order to achieve a speedy improvement that avoids state force.' 4. The state does not punish many vices which damage the church and have to be criticized by the church."[116]

Martin Luther's 'two kingdoms doctrine' played a central role in the separation of (and solidarity with, in the final event) the two covenantal institutions of church and state. In my opinion we actually need a 'four kingdom doctrine,' whereby we could draw upon Luther. The relationship between the church and the state has long stood in the center of attention, but the relationship of these entities to the economy and the family is also of importance. In Christian ethics we have to rethink the relationship not only about the two creation ordinances, but rather how the four creation ordinances relate to each other. Perhaps we are nowadays more aware of the relationship between the family and the state or between the economy

---

[116] Erdmann K. Sturm. Der junge Zacharias Ursin: Sein Weg vom Philippismus zum Calvinismus. Beiträge zur Geschichte und Lehre der Reformierten Kirche 33. Neukirchener Verlag: Neukirchen, 1972. pp. 307-308 (instances are also indicated there).

and the state than earlier generations. However, the Bible prescribes ethics on this topic, about which many thoughts throughout church history have been produced.

The mandates belong together

Because all covenants in God's created order are subordinate to God, they have to be mindful of the mandates of the other covenants. The covenants reciprocally help each other, insofar as they do not overstep their own duties and rights. The church prays for the authorities, advises them, and admonishes its members to respect the state. Parents raise their children to respect the authority willed by God – also in the other covenants. The economy and the family finance the state and the church by their taxes and gifts. The church in turn assists parents to raise their children according to the will of God.

None of the four mandates is to come under the rule of another, and none of the mandates can exist independently of the other. And yet in certain aspects every mandate is subordinate to the authority of the other mandates.

Every person simultaneously belongs within the four creation mandates. Through that alone it is apparent that the four mandates are not independent of each other. Everyone can and must differentiate between his duties and authority within the four categories, but he still remains *one* person. I can thus be a father, a member of a church council, and politically engaged all at the same time. On the one hand, I have to keep these duties and responsibilities separate from each other. On the other hand, the very fact that I am one and the same person sees to it that the different categories interact.

The family has its own duties and responsibilities as well as rights. It does not receive these from the state. Rather they precede the state.[117] And nevertheless, the state should not only promote the family, but rather it should also enact laws that define the beginning and the end of a family. It is therefore legal in the case of incessant child abuse for the state to withdraw from the parents the right to raise children. From the preset authority of the family, it follows that only the state can take action against the abuse of family authority.

There is also the danger that a mandate will seek to rule over another mandate and not accept its sovereignty. On the other hand, there is also the

---

[117] Comp. J. B. Shearer. Hebrew Institutions. Presbyterian Committee of Publication: Richmond (VI), 1910. pp. 11-13.

great danger that a single mandate develops a life of its own, which denies the interrelatedness of the mandates.

How can this be conveyed to a Secular Environment?
When someone wants to make a good and sensible decision, that person has to know his duty within the authority structure in which he finds himself. The basic institutions of our society do not derive their basis for existence from each other. Rather, they have their dignity and function within themselves. Each of them has certain duties and with them authority, and yet each of them is restricted in their duties and authority and has to respect the duties and rights of other institutions.

The four ethical institutions (mandates)

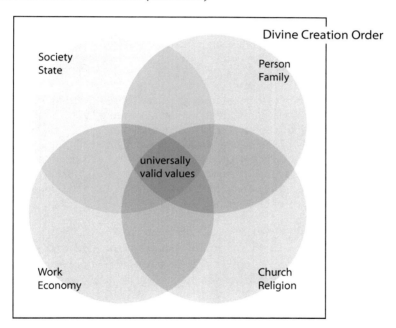

Illustration by Karl Schock, according to Dietrich Bonhoeffer and Thomas Schirrmacher

Examples of the dangers of overstepping the boundaries of individual mandates

The same value that is valid for all areas of life can be expressed quite differently within the framework of a particular area of life. Also, a particular area of life is backed up by various task groupings. For this reason, it is important that one know one's field of responsibility. In contrast, whoever mixes the scope of duties will destroy the freedom of the individual areas of life.

Example from the business sector

> As an employer I cannot treat an employee as I would my child, because I am dealing with an adult. This adult is under my control only insofar as the labor contract addresses it.

Example from family life

> By the same token, I cannot treat my child as I would an employee and 'lay off' my child after numerous warnings. Even when I want to raise my child to cooperate, I have no claim on a concrete level of job performance. It is correct that child labor is forbidden.

Example from church life

> The church is prohibited by God from using any form of force in order to assert its interests within and without the church, regardless of how justified these interests might appear. The church indeed supports the monopoly of force in the hands of the state. However, it is for this very reason that the church does not have any sort of possibility of asserting its opinion by physical or psychological force. Its weapon is solely the 'word,' that is to say, the possibility of convincing others. In the extreme case it can exclude its members, but otherwise its hands are tied.

How can this be conveyed to a secular environment?
It would be going too far to present all dangers associated with overstepping the boundaries of a mandate, but some examples should be outlined in order to elucidate the scope of the subject matter.

The family dominates the church: There were times in the Middle Ages when a pope's blood relationships dominated large portions of the church.

The family dominates the economy: In some countries in Latin America very large fortunes were amassed in the families of first born children via inheritance rights, who then as large land owners controlled the country's economy.

The family dominates the state: In the history of mankind it has often been families, mostly aristocratic families, who have dominated the state. Saudi Arabia is a modern-day example of this situation.

The church/religion dominates the state: For a long time the pope laid claim to the right to appoint the emperor (The Investitures Conflict) and to

2. Normative decisions

have a voice in all important political decisions. Iran is a modern example for the dependence of the state on religious leaders ("Mullah regime").

The church dominates the family: Over the course of church history, it has occasionally been the case that the church has limited or controlled freedoms in child rearing.

The state dominates the family: In communistic (or fascist) states, families were at times forced to comply with certain methods or goals for child rearing. Educational socialism can be named in this case.

The state dominates the church: At times in the Byzantine Empire, there was "Caesaropapism," meaning a church-state legal system in which the worldly ruler was the head of the church. That a minister is the "highest lord of the church" also applies to a completely different time in the Prussian state up to 1919 (and 1945, respectively). In some European monarchies (e.g., England and The Netherlands), the queen is still today the formal church 'head.'

The state dominates the economy: Socialism and communism provide numerous examples for this situation. At the same time, excessive bureaucracy in present day democracies robs the economy of numerous freedoms at its own expense.[118]

The economy dominates the church: In European history, financial transfers often determined the choice of bishops and other ecclesiastical dignitaries. One could think of the influence of the Fugger banking family with respect to who filled ecclesiastical offices. The Reformation was in part a reaction to this situation. Even today, from time to time there are large donors who have an important influence on churches.

The economy dominates the state: In the USA, for example, the cost of campaigning for the Presidency of the United States is such an expensive and 'privately' financed proposition that it could not take place without substantial donations coming from large donors. In Switzerland banks largely 'determine' politics (consider the bankruptcy of Swissair).

---

[118] In particular Werner Lachmann. "Interdependenzen von marktwirtschaftlichen und demokratischen Systemen." pp. 37-50 in: Reinhard Haupt, Werner Lachmann (ed.). Selbstorganisation in Markt und Management. Hänssler: Neuhausen, 1995, here pp. 44-48, as well as the historical example provided by Gerd Habermann. "Der Untergang Roms: Ein ordnungspolitisches Lehrstück." Orientierungen zur Wirtschafts- und Gesellschaftspolitik [Ludwig-Erhard-Stiftung] 40 (June 1989): 53-57. Comp. additionally Elisabeth Noelle-Neumann. "Ein freiheitliches Wirtschaftssystem macht die Gesellschaft glücklicher." Frankfurter Allgemeine Zeitung dated November 3, 1999 (No. 256). pp. W1-W2; Werner Lachmann, Reinhard Haupt, Karl Framer (ed.). Erneuerung der Sozialen Marktwirtschaft: Chancen und Risiken. Marktwirtschaft und Ethik 3. Lit Verlag: Münster, 1996; Walter Künneth. Moderne Wirtschaft – Christliche Existenz. Claudius: München, 1959.

The economy dominates the family: Particularly in the 19th century, the economy determined the life of working families in such a way that family life in the sense we know it today can hardly be spoken of ("Manchester Capitalism").

3. Deciding Situationally

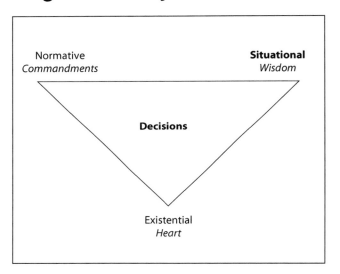

3.1. Leading situationally means balancing pros and cons and calculating the possible outcome

From normative to situational ethics

We have just seen that the normative side of ethics and decision making presses towards the situational side of things in a rather formal manner. This is due to the fact that normative ethics is a principled ethic that only provides a framework for life. This is expressed in biblical commands, which cannot be thought of independently of any concrete person or situation.

Example from the church sector

> Timothy is called upon (1 Timothy 5:1-2) to admonish an older man in pastoral counseling as he would a father, a young man as a brother, an older lady as a mother, and a younger lady as a sister. This command can only be

3. Deciding Situationally

carried over to today if an individual expressly knows who is in front of him and knows how an individual deals with fathers and brothers in our culture. If every person and each Christian so employs his gifts and abilities as God has made him (e.g., Romans 12:3-8; 1 Peter 4: 7-8), it is not enough to simply know the command. In fact, a sound knowledge of individuals also has to be present in order to put the command found in 1 Peter 4:10 ("Each one should use whatever gift he has received ...") into practice. God does not call upon anyone to evangelize on a grand scale if he has not received the gift of an evangelist. How often would a bad conscience be produced – unnecessarily – if a particular gift or service were made to be a standard for all church members?

The Bible sees itself as the fountainhead of ethics and at the same time calls for taking explicit situations from experience into account. The wisdom literature of the Bible offers many good examples of this. Still, before we occupy ourselves with it, we want to first address norm conflicts. This is due to the fact that in an explicit situation various values and commands come into conflict with each other, and at that point it becomes clear that the best values cannot have an effect without tangible application.

Ethical conflict

That the values that protect God's commands have a ranking, and correspondingly that a transgression of the commands receive differing weightings, becomes clear when two commands come into conflict with each other. Catholic theology speaks at this point about a "collision of duties."[119]

How can this be conveyed to a secular environment?
In an ivory tower one can discuss every command and every value detached from reality and quickly come to solutions. In reality, however, there is a flood of questions that simultaneously assail us, and we find ourselves placed before numerous values at the same time. The question is often not which values we wish to pursue, but rather in which order we do them justice. Questions of priority presuppose a ranking of values that does not just answer what is in itself good and what is not, but rather challenges us with the question of what has priority.

---

[119] See, for example, Karl Hörmann. Lexikon der christlichen Moral. Tyrolia: Innsbruck, 1976.² Cols. 1281-1284 ("collision of duties [*Pflichtenkollision*]").

For example

> The most famous example in the Bible is surely the statement that Peter makes to the Jewish authorities, who want to prohibit him and the Apostles from proclaiming the gospel: "We must obey God rather than men!" (Acts 5:29). Previously the Apostle had already challenged his interrogators: "Judge for yourselves whether it is right in God's sight to obey you rather than God" (Acts 4:19). Here the divine command to proclaim the gospel stands above the divine command to obey the authorities. Daniel's three friends behaved similarly when they did not follow Nebuchadnezzar's order to worship a religious statue (Daniel 3). Daniel changed nothing in his prayer practice in the face of Darius' command, which ultimately brought him into the lion's den (Daniel 6). The prohibition against idolatry was more important to Daniel than the duty to obey the state. In these examples we are not primarily dealing with a basic rejection of state authority. Peter and the other Apostles otherwise held to s*tate directives. The conflict first arose when the state demands ran counter to a higher command.*
>
> An example from today would be the following: if the state demands taxes from me, I pay them. If, however, the state demands that I participate in an abortion, I would resist.

In this example, by the way, it becomes clear that a collision of obligations can very easily arise between the four basic institutions of family, church, the economy, and the state. This can be due to the fact that we have to decide which particular area has priority at the moment, or because (as in our example) an area too deeply invades the authority of another and endangers its values (in our example the basic duty of the church to proclaim the gospel or the family giving birth to life).

The example of lying to save life

A frequent conflict has to do with the two commands not to murder and not to lie, that is to say, the fifth and sixth commandments. Since the command to protect life is higher than the command not to lie, in the case of a conflict a lie is allowed to save life.[120] This is first and foremost visible in the

---

[120] Excellent presentations relating hereto are by Helmut Thielicke. Theologische Ethik. 2. Bd. 1. Teil: Mensch und Welt. J. C. B. Mohr: Tübingen, 1959². pp. 122-127; Robert L. Dabney. Systematic Theology. The Banner of Truth Trust: Edinburgh, 1985 (1875² reprint). pp. 424-426; Jim West. "Rahab's Justifiable Lie." pp. 66-74 in: Gary North (ed.). The Theology of Christian Resistance. Christianity and Civilization 2. Geneva Divinity School Press: Tyler (TX), 1983 (comp. with the entire volume); Rousas J. Rushdoony. Institutes of Biblical Law. Presbyterian and Reformed: Phillipsburg (NJ), 1973. pp. 542-549; Rousas J. Rushdoony. Intellectu-

3. Deciding Situationally

case of the prostitute Rahab which is mentioned again and again, although there are many examples in the Old Testament.[121] The lie to save life became one of the most frequently discussed ethical problems in church history.[122] When Luther appealed to lying in order to save life[123] (a view that was later discarded from Lutheran theology), he reaped intense criticism from the Catholic Church. The Catholic Church is indeed aware of decisions made in favor of a higher command, but in the case of lying did not apply it.

Lies to save lives

- Exodus 1:15-21: God "blesses" the midwives (verse 20), because they do not obey the order of the Pharaoh to kill all Hebrew infants and want to placate him with a lie.
- Exodus 2:3-9: (in particular verses 8-9): Moses' mother Jochebed, as well as her daughter and Moses' sister Miriam, conceal their blood relationship with Moses when he is found by the daughter of the Pharaoh in a papyrus basket in the Nile, so that Moses was given back, so that Jochebed became a wet nurse for her own son.
- Joshua 2:1-22: The prostitute Rahab deceives the king of Jericho by indicating that the Israelite spies have already left and thereby saves both their and her life. She does this because she believes in the God of Israel. In Hebrews 11:31 she is viewed as a heroine of the faith. In James 2:25 this is affirmatively mentioned: "In the same way, was not even Rahab the prostitute considered righteous for what she did when she gave lodging to the spies and sent them off in a different direction?"

---

al Schizophrenia, Culture, Crisis and Education. Presbyterian and Reformed: Philadelphia (PA), 1961. pp. 79-80.

[121] Compare the examples by Axel Denecke. Wahrhaftigkeit: Eine evangelische Kasuistik. Vandenhoeck & Ruprecht, Göttingen, 1971. pp. 246-249.

[122] The classical presentation from the Catholic point of view regarding this controversial point is by Gregor Müller. Die Wahrhaftigkeitspflicht und die Problematik der Lüge. Freiburger Theologische Studien 78. Herder: Freiburg, 1962, which reports on countless theologians, among which many represent my position, e.g., pp. 212, 274-275, 325 (No. 1-2, 4-5) and 326-327 (No. 9-10, 12) and 330-331 (No. 1) and 332-334 (No. 3, 7-9, 15) 327 (No.12) and 344 (No.9). Axel Denecke. Wahrhaftigkeit. op. cit., pp. 166-186 offers a history of the rejection of the white lie, in particular as seen by Augustine and St. Thomas Aquinas, and demonstrating, however, that most representatives of the stance were in practice much less consistent than in theory.

[123] Axel Denecke. Wahrhaftigkeit. op. cit., pp. 251-253; William Walker Rockwell. Die Doppelehe des Landgrafen Philipp von Hessen. N. G. Elwert'sche Verlagsbuchhandlung: Marburg, 1904. pp. 178-180.

- Psalm 34: "A Psalm of David when he feigned madness before Abimelech, who drove him away and he departed" (comp. 1 Samuel 21:10-15). (David feigned madness so that his enemy Abimelech would not kill him.)
- 1 Samuel 16:2: Upon God's command Samuel disguises his intentions by bringing a sacrifice, so that Saul will not kill him (comp. commentary in this text to this section of Scripture).
- 1 Samuel 19:9-17: David's wife Michal saves David's and her life from Saul by lying.
- 2 Samuel 17:18-21: A woman saves the lives of David's spies from Absalom by lying.

The legal adages from the Middle Ages that "necessity knows no law," that "necessity and death know no law," and "necessity looks for bread wherever it can be found" basically summarizes that many commands may be transgressed when it has to do with an emergency situation and in particular to preventing the endangerment of life.[124]

The example of the Sabbath command

An additional example of the conflict of divine commands is the prohibition against work on the Sabbath and many other commands that also apply to the Sabbath but do not have anything to do with work. Jesus healed on the Sabbath[125] and asked: "'Which is lawful on the Sabbath: to do good or to do evil, to save life or to kill?' But they remained silent" (Mark 3:4). They responded in this manner because the scribes knew exactly that this was not forbidden in the Old Testament. In Matthew 12:11-12 Jesus asks similarly: "If any of you has a sheep and it falls into a pit on the Sabbath, will you not take hold of it and lift it out? How much more valuable is a man than a sheep! Therefore it is lawful to do good on the Sabbath" (comp Luke 14:5). Saving animals on the Sabbath was also naturally allowed in Old Testament times. In Luke 13:15 Jesus refers to the commonly allowed practice of giving water to oxen and donkeys on the Sabbath.

In Mark 2:23-28 (similarly Matthew 12:1-7; Luke 6:1-5) Jesus justifies his disciples' picking heads of grain with a reference to David, who when starving was allowed to eat the showbread in the temple (1 Samuel 21:4-7).

---

[124] Rechtssprichwörter und sprichwörtliche Redensarten mit rechtlichem Inhalt. Mittelalterliches Kriminalmuseum; Rothenburg ob der Tauber, 1992. p. 78.

[125] He healed: a man with a shriveled hand Matthew 12:8-14 as in Mark 3:1-6 as in Luke 6:6-11; a weak woman: Luke 13:10-17; a man suffering from dropsy: Luke 14:1-6; a man at the pool of Bethesda: John 5:1-18; also comp. John 7:21-24.

3. Deciding Situationally

In John 7:23 Jesus says: "Now if a child can be circumcised on the Sabbath so that the law of Moses may not be broken, why are you angry with me for healing the whole man on the Sabbath?" The command to survive and the circumcision command were more important than the Sabbath command. In Matthew 12:5 Jesus asks: "Or haven't you read in the Law that on the Sabbath the priests in the temple desecrate the day and yet are innocent?" Jesus names examples of biblical commands in all these texts (service of priests, circumcision, saving life, watering animals, etc.) that are higher than the Sabbath command. This is made particularly clear in Matthew 12:5, since Jesus expressly says that in their action the priests "desecrate" and yet are "innocent."

In the Old Testament there are additional exceptions to the Sabbath command that show how it is to be understood correctly and how many of God's commands were higher than the Sabbath command. The royal bodyguards were active on the Sabbath with the approval of the high priest (2 Kings 11:5-9) and even changed on the Sabbath.

It goes without saying that sacrifices were made on the Sabbath in Old Testament times (even the usual sacrifices: Numbers 28:10), and there were many festive days with numerous and work-intensive sacrifices. There were also nonrecurring celebrations such as the dedication of Solomon's temple (1 Kings 8:64-65; 2 Chronicles 7:7-9), which occurred on the Sabbath. Showbread was set out on the Sabbath (Leviticus 24:8; 1 Chronicles 9:32), and it was on the Sabbath that the divisions of priests and Levites changed their assignments (2 Chronicles 23:4, 8). The Sabbath was clearly the most work intensive day of the week for the priests and Levites.

Jesus therefore did not oppose the Sabbath command. Rather, by weighing different responsibilities and drawing sensible conclusions in the case of similarly supported examples, and by appealing to common sense, he gave back to the Sabbath its correct significance and place.

Regarding the justification of deciding in favor of a higher command

Reformed theology[126] reckons that in each situation where a decision is made and where God's commands collide with each other, there can be a correct decision because everyone is obligated to the higher command. In each case the higher command constitutes an exception over against the

---

[126] Comp, e.g., John M. Frame. The Doctrine of the Knowledge of God: A Theology of Lordship. Presbyterian & Reformed: Phillipsburg (NJ), 1987. pp. 137-139 "Hierarchies of Norms."

lower command.[127] This appears to me to be appropriate given the mentioned examples and the fact that biblical commands assume that an individual can do what is right and good in each situation. I know of no example in the Bible where someone was in a situation where a decision had to be made and the individual had to sin no matter what the course of action. That is to say, the decision could only be made in a manner where there was a less weighty sin. In the examples named that have to do with 'lies to save life,' it is my view that there was no guilt present. Otherwise, these people would not have been able to have been placed before us as paragons of faith.

In contrast, Lutheran theology reckons that man always becomes guilty in such a conflict, but it holds the more important command to be decisive. For this reason, Lutheran theology refers to the "lesser evil." For instance, Walter Künneth considers killing a tyrant like Hitler a boundary situation to be justifiable. He also believes, however, that the active subject needs forgiveness for guilt.[128] Hans-Josef Wilting has correctly emphasized that this Lutheran viewpoint is associated with the idea that as a sinner an individual (this applies to Christians as well) cannot truly correctly do anything anyway.[129] This Lutheran viewpoint does not concord with Luther himself. For instance, Luther did not view a 'white lie' in light of a risk to one's life or in an emergency to be a sin, at which point he was in conflict with the Catholic theology of his time.[130]

---

[127] Non-Reformed Theologians also represent this view, for instance Norman L. Geisler. "Graded Absolutism." pp. 131-137 in: David K. Clark, Robert V. Rakestraw. Readings in Christian Ethics. Vol. 1: Theory and Method. Baker Books: Grand Rapids, 1994; Norman L. Geisler. Christian Ethics. Baker: Grand Rapids, 1989. pp. 116-122 and more often.

[128] Walter Künneth. Der Christ als Staatsbürger. TVG. R. Brockhaus: Wuppertal, 1984. p. 96. The most extensive presentation oft his position is found in Helmut Thielicke. Theologische Ethik. Vol. 2: Entfaltung, Part 1: Mensch und Welt. J. C. B. Mohr: Tübingen, 1959.² pp. 56-327.

[129] Comp. Martin Honecker. Einführung in die Theologische Ethik. Walter de Gruyter: Berlin, 1990. p. 238 und Hans-Josef Wilting. Der Kompromiß als theologisches und als ethisches Problem. Patmos: Düsseldorf: 1975. pp. 11-46 regarding the Lutheran Helmut Thielicke und pp. 47-64 regarding the Lutheraner Wolfgang Trillhaas. Surprisingly, Wilting only discusses more recent Lutheran theologians, for which reason other conceptions of the collision of obligations are not even addressed.

[130] Also in Axel Denecke. Wahrhaftigkeit. op.cit., pp. 251-253 and William Walker Rockwell. Die Doppelehe des Landgrafen Philipp von Hessen. op.cit., pp. 178-180.

3. Deciding Situationally

Georg Huntemann sees in such case how Lutheran theology is confronted with a true conflict[131] that "can never be solved."[132] "Every true conflict has its cause in the conflicting nature of the world."[133] A Christian, however, should not break to pieces in the face of such a conflict. Rather, a Christian should "overcome" it.[134] Nevertheless, such a conflict cannot "be overcome without guilt and forgiveness."[135] Subsequent to Bonhoeffer, he calls this "assumption of guilt" a responsible and conscious acceptance of guilt.

All of these views assume that an individual, in the case of a collision of obligations, always basically becomes guilty and/or has to wait for a special, situation-specific command from God. In my opinion this does arise in the examples named from the Bible. Rather, they are advanced developments of respective theological systems that do not permit any other choice if an internal contradiction is not to arise. From my point of view, there is no evidence indicating that a Christian can get into a situation in which he no longer can do good and do the will of God and rather sins one way or the other. I know of no attempt to reconcile the view that an ethical conflict makes sin unavoidable with the concrete biblical narratives in which on the basis of one command another cannot be performed. Was it truly sin – even if a smaller one – when Peter refused to obey the authorities as otherwise required by God, because he wanted to obey God more than men and because for him the Great Commission was above obedience to the authorities?

To speak of a 'lesser evil' should, for that reason, be given up altogether.[136] Peter's disobedience over against the state or the work of a priest on the Sabbath was no 'lesser' evil. Rather it is no evil at all. No new confession-based quarrels should arise as a result of this. Even if I hold the Reformed view to be more stringent, from Lutheran and Catholic points of view the solution of a collision of duties should be decided in favor of the higher duty.

---

[131] Georg Huntemann. Der verlorene Maßstab: Gottes Gebot im Chaos dieser Zeit. VLM: Bad Liebenzell, 1983. pp. 110-126 (emphasis is left out in the following).

[132] Ibid., p. 112.

[133] Ibid., p. 111.

[134] Ibid., p. 112.

[135] Ibid., p. 116; literally the same as in Georg Huntemann. Biblisches Ethos im Zeitalter der Moralrevolution. Hänssler: Neuhausen, 1996. p. 169.

[136] So also in Karl Hörmann. Lexikon der christlichen Moral. Tyrolia: Innsbruck, 1976². Cols. 892-894 ("Kleineres Übel").

Example from church life

Many churches are confronted with the question: What is the appropriate form of worship service that equally serves young people as well as older people? Sound judgment and willingness to compromise are required in the situation. The most important value, however, is that we serve God with all our heart, and that we not only do that externally. What is decisive is also that we not serve other gods or serve ourselves. Furthermore, the gospel should be proclaimed in a way that people understand it and that no unnecessary cultural barriers are placed before them (1 Corinthians 9:19-22). Certain elements that cannot be dispensed with are, however, 'tabu' and have priority in every collision of obligations. For this reason we are not able to simply do away with the Lord's Supper just because it is difficult for our contemporaries to understand. In many other questions, however, we can completely adapt to people, if such adaptation does not do away with a command of God. We do this almost 'automatically' if we use the language of our listeners and not 'the language of Canaan.' And then there is still a large area left. This has to do with basic values (e.g., music that glorifies God), whereby we have to adapt to our listeners in order to follow the command to enter into their world (1 Corinthians 9:19-22). This means that we have to find a musical style that caters to (all!) visitors and church members, or we have to change the music style and adapt to the respective listenership.

Example from the state sector

The question of embryonic stem cell research is a good example of a collision of duties. On the one side there is the (inviolable) dignity of the individual, or concretely: the dignity of the embryo. On the other side there are the following, likewise basic and important values: 1. The freedom to conduct research, 2. The potential to (possibly) be able to heal diseases that have heretofore been incurable, 3. The opportunity to earn money. These three values are basically to be fostered. In a collision of duties associated with the (inviolable) human dignity of an embryo, these values, which are in themselves important, have to be waived. This is the case even if the freedom to conduct research is restricted, incurable diseases thereby possible remain incurable, and no money can be earned.

Example from the business sector

It is a basic aspect of economic theory that the state cannot simultaneously achieve all its goals by means of good economic policies. High economic growth, low inflation, low unemployment, and a marginal gap between rich and poor are in themselves all good goals and apply reasonable values. And 'as a long wish list' each of these goals is to be aspired to. In reality, a specialist in the area of economics, as well as a politician, is no prophet and is additionally confronted with the problem that a massive bias toward only one goal can endanger the others. Only a most extensive balance of all goals and continuous examination of whether one of the goals is being left behind enables an economic policy that is for the good of all. Moreover, every good economic decision, regardless of how good it might be, can only try to keep all factors in view. One has to live with the fact that after a considerable time, other elements have to be brought into play.

Example from family life

Christian ethics, in the absolute prohibition against abortion, has always seen an exception to be the situation where the life of the mother is endangered. Since only an equally significant value, or a more highly estimated value, can permit an exception to a command, the command to protect the life of the unborn can only be opposed in the case of a threat to the life of another (concretely: a threat to the life of the mother). The mother's financial situation or health problems (as lower categorized values) are not allowed to be decisive. The decision is difficult in the case where the life of the child *or* the life of the mother is at risk, since here there are two equal values pitted against each other. (Only very rarely will a doctor be able to make such an explicit prognosis.) An obvious exception to the prohibition against abortion is present if either mother *and* child or only the child would have to die.[137] Generally this is the case in a tubal pregnancy. For this reason, Christian ethics have seldom had any objection against ending a tubular pregnancy or similar cases. Because it is all too often forgotten to give a precise ethical justification for such action, such decisions are mostly seen as inconsistent.

Example from the business sector

> A company is experiencing sluggish orders. Which values come into play at this point? Keeping jobs is one value. Maintaining the company as a going concern is another. The latter is indeed a precondition for maintaining jobs. Furthermore, among the employees there are some that have been extremely loyal to the company and in their efforts have gone far beyond that which was necessary. It is a difficult balancing of interests to think about whether and whom to lay off in order to keep the company operating and at least to ensure some jobs. No one is pleased to make such a decision. If a way opens to avoid the problem by, for example, receiving additional orders, everyone has reason for joy. As long as this is not the case, one basic balancing of in-

---

[137] Also in Karl Barth. Die Kirchliche Dogmatik. Vol. 3. 4. Part. op. cit., pp. 479-481, as well as John Jefferson Davis. Abortion and the Christian. op. cit., p. 71 as well as the numerous Evangelical authors to which he refers.

terests remains to limit the overall damage and preserve as much employment as possible.

How can this be conveyed to a secular environment?
Whoever is without a canon of values does not have any pros and cons to weigh. However, it is also the case that whoever holds to a certain cadre of values has to have a hierarchy of values and an appreciation for deciding in the face of conflict. Certain values are normally inviolable, and on account of this certain actions are tabu. Still, there are other values that come in under the threshold of 'inviolability' that can be regarded in a trade-off. For this reason the balancing of interests is not a watering down of values and goals. Rather, it is a necessary condition for a good decision that serves as many people as possible.

Deciding without prophecy

Among other reasons, balancing interests is necessary because we are not prophets. We do not know what tomorrow will bring and which unforeseen factors could frustrate our calculations. We can only regard our present knowledge and perhaps what we suspect to be the case. Hindsight is 20-20. Unfortunately, decisions always have to be taken before we know more. Perhaps we can learn some things for the next similar situation but not for the past.

Sometimes one wishes that in life there was a 'rewind button' like there is on a computer keyboard. When I choose a font, I look at the result. If I do not like it, I go back to what I had. That would be the way to work out decisions. If we do not like what we see, we rewind. But God has made us so that we have to decide on the basis of available values and knowledge. In doing so we should indeed have some thoughts about what consequences our decisions will bring. In many areas we can play through the future in our mind or try a computer simulation. Still, we are responsible to God and our conscience for every decision made, and we do this without knowing the precise results and without being able to rescind the decisions.

Even as Christians we can also make poor decisions and – if they are tied to sin and guilt – admit them and have them forgiven. This should be easier for Christians than for others. A Christian knows that in the center of his faith is a certainty that Jesus paid for his mistakes and guilt by dying for him a long time ago. A Christian knows that no one is inerrant and that admitting mistakes never has to be the end. Rather, it is the opportunity for a new start.

3. Deciding Situationally 93

In the secular domain

No set of ethics can get along without balancing interests, that is to say, without a position that attributes different rankings to various values and, in the case of a collision of duties, gives priority to a higher value. This means: "The theory of balancing interests forms the centerpiece of every ethical system."[138]

Example from the state sector

Criminal law cannot get along without a) hierarchy of laws, and 2) without clarification on what to do in the case of a conflict. Whoever acts in self-defense does not "act in opposition to the law" and "acts without bringing guilt upon himself."[139] This is correct and is according to the German penal code, which allows behavior in the case of an emergency that is otherwise prohibited. If a house is on fire, one is allowed to break windows to save people. This is otherwise viewed as burglary and destruction of property. Herbert Tröndle writes in a commentary on penal law: "A collision of duties is present when an individual is confronted with multiple, mutually exclusive legal obligations and, in a concrete situation, that individual has to objectively choose in favor of a higher obligation to the detriment of the lower one."[140] A different commentary on the penal code defines this at more length but just as fittingly (which also applies to Christian ethics in general): "If two (or more) legal precepts of a manner arise, such that only either one or the other can be fulfilled (a true collision of duties), the individual addressee of these norms[141] is to fulfill the higher precept in the case of differing valuations and is to fulfill one of the precepts in the case of equal valuations. To not fulfill the other precept or precepts is not unlawful."[142] "If there is a conflict involving two objects of legal protection where no alternative

---

[138] Rupert Lay. Ethik für Manager. Econ Taschenbuch Verlag: Düsseldorf, 1996. p. 85; comp. pp. 121-133; also comp. Robert Alexy. "Güter- und Übelabwägung, 1. Rechtlich." pp. 181-182 und Stephan Feldhaus. "Güter- und Übelabwägung, 2. Ethisch." pp. 182-190 in: Lexikon der Bioethik. 3 Vols. Vol. 2. Gütersloher Verlagshaus: Gütersloh, 1998 (contains a good bibliography).

[139] Strafgesetzbuch § 32-34 zitiert nach Strafgesetzbuch ... Deutscher Taschenbuch Verlag: München, 1991.^{25} p. 22 (§ 34 and 35).

[140] Herbert Tröndle. Strafgesetzbuch und Nebengesetze. C. H. Beck: München, 1997.^{48} p. 210 ("Vor § 32", margin number 11).

[141] That is to say the affected party, the agent.

[142] Hans Joachim Hirsch. "Zweiter Abschnitt: Die Tat: Vor § 32." pp. 1-118 in: Hans-Heinrich Jeschek, Wolfgang Ruß, Günther Willms (Hg.). Strafgesetzbuch: Leipziger Kommentar: Großkommentar. Vol. 2: §§ 32 to 60. Walter de Gruyter: Berlin, 1985.^{10} p. 41 (margin number 71).

exists to destroying or damaging one or the other such object, then the object of less value has to yield to the object of higher value. Encroachment upon the object of less value is not unlawful."[143] "Correspondingly, to not follow the higher precept is unlawful if the individual fulfills the lesser precept instead."[144]

(Incidentally, the difference between a normal collision of duties and an emergency lies in the fact that the collision of duties does not presuppose that the object of legal protection is in acute danger.[145])

In my opinion the collision of duties is more often a part of 'everyday business' than is normally assumed. This is because every single day every individual has to weigh up which obligations he or she will fulfill and in which order this will be done.

The existence of the four basic institutions leads to this situation. When I get up in the morning, I have to decide how I am going to fulfill my obligations as a husband and father, pastor, employer and citizen. Most of the time I cannot fulfill all the obligations simultaneously, and yet all of them are mandates received from God. I am therefore continually conducting a balancing of interests. Under normal circumstances we have enough time at our disposal to fulfill the various obligations, and the consequences of our decisions are not normally dramatic. It is not until extreme circumstances such as a threat to life come into play that we become painfully aware of what it means to weigh various interests.

Example from the business sector

Work and relaxation are also divine mandates, whereby the basic division foresees six days of work and one day of rest. Still, there are obligations to be weighed against each other, when I work for money and when I work voluntarily, when I rest and when I sleep and in which relationship these things stand to each other. No one says that balancing these interests occurs easily and indiscernibly. Large portions of our appointment books reflect the attempt to cope with numerous tasks and to avoid or resolve conflicts.

---

[143] Hans Joachim Hirsch. "Zweiter Abschnitt: Die Tat: Rechtfertigender Notstand § 34." pp. 1-118 in: Hans-Heinrich Jeschek, Wolfgang Ruß, Günther Willms (ed.). Strafgesetzbuch: Leipziger Kommentar: Großkommentar. Vol. 2: §§ 32 to 60. Walter de Gruyter: Berlin, 1985.^{10} p. 120.

[144] Hans Joachim Hirsch. "Zweiter Abschnitt: Die Tat: Vor § 32." pp. 1-118 in: Hans-Heinrich Jeschek, Wolfgang Ruß, Günther Willms (Hg.). Strafgesetzbuch: Leipziger Kommentar: Großkommentar. Vol. 2: §§ 32 to 60. Walter de Gruyter: Berlin, 1985.^{10} p. 44 (margin number 78).

[145] Ibid., p. 42 (margin number 75); comp. Herbert Tröndle. Strafgesetzbuch und Nebengesetze. op. cit., pp. 205-236.

3. Deciding Situationally

Example from the family sector

Whoever goes shopping and deliberates whether to spend money for this or for that important item, and thereby considers which other financial responsibilities he has, is weighing various interests in a collision of obligations. Perhaps whoever has enough money experiences a collision of obligations less often than someone who has less money at his disposal and therefore has to decide the things with which he has to dispense. The financial collision of obligations soon becomes apparent in the use of family household means. What is available to be put to use to finance which items? What is the relationship between my spending in order to be able to work, to the expenses for my marriage partner or family? If a welfare recipient gives the priority to feeding his or her children at the expense of feeding himself, the obligation collision is resolved in a selfless manner. But sooner or later he has to find a different solution so that he himself does not suffer a loss of his health. This would in turn be devastating for the children.

Obligation collisions and compromises

Wolfgang Trillhaas defines the difference between a collision of duties and a compromise[146] as follows: "A compromise is a freely made agreement by which there is a mutual relinquishment of certain interests in order to ensure a higher common good."[147] In a compromise it is not two commands that oppose each other, but rather two different, legitimate interests that have to be reconciled with each other.[148] Our entire everyday life as well as most societal questions consist of such trade-offs. If both interests in themselves are not reprehensible, then what is impending is a wise decision that reconciles both sides so that the greatest possible benefit is achieved for each party. If one of the positions represented is morally objectionable, a compromise is not permissible.

It is possible that in such a situation an individual is dealing with a collision of duties: how do I achieve a legitimate goal if immoral interests follow, and these, however, cannot be gotten around nor turned around? In a

---

[146] The concept of compromise is, however, often used in a confusing manner to comprehensively express all types of collisions of obligations, for instance in Hans-Josef Wilting. Der Kompromiß als theologisches und als ethisches Problem. Patmos: Düsseldorf: 1975. Comp. to the differentiations in Martin Honecker. Einführung in die Theologische Ethik. Walter de Gruyter: Berlin, 1990. pp. 234-243 "Kompromiß und Güterabwägung im Normenkonflikt."

[147] Wolfgang Trillhaas. "Kompromiß." Evangelisches Staatslexikon. 1966.¹ Cols. 1113-1116, here Col. 1114.

[148] Comp with Axel Denecke. Wahrhaftigkeit: Eine evangelische Kasuistik. Vandenhoeck & Ruprecht, Göttingen, 1971 aufgeführten Beispiele bei Paulus.

following section entitled "How to respond to Sin?" we will deal with this issue.

Bigger and smaller sins?

In Matthew 5:17-20 Jesus says that he did not come to do away with the Old Testament law, but that rather he wanted to fulfill it. In this connection we read in Matthew 5:19: "Anyone who breaks one of the least of these commandments and teaches others to do the same will be called least in the kingdom of heaven, but whoever practices and teaches these commands will be called great in the kingdom of heaven."[149] From this it is apparent that for Jesus there were more and less important commands.

Commands are major when they presuppose and defend a greater value. The Pharisees often took the more minor commands very seriously but they "neglected the more important matters of the law." For this reason, in his critique of the Pharisees Jesus gives the following warning: "Woe to you, teachers of the law and Pharisees, you hypocrites! You give a tenth of your spices – mint, dill and cumin. But you have neglected the more important matters of the law – justice, mercy and faithfulness. You should have practiced the latter, without neglecting the former. You blind guides! You strain out a gnat but swallow a camel" (Matthew 23:23-24). *The lesser values are by all means to be considered, but only after the higher values have been allowed for.*

The severity of a sin, and with it the priority of the value that has been violated, is often seen in the degree of penalty. In the Old Testament, for example, the highest sentence was given to adultery (Leviticus 20:10; Deuteronomy 22:20-23). However, sex before marriage was not punishable by death unless it was by incest. Incest received the severest penalty (Leviticus 20:11-17). In the case of premarital sex between people who were not at least 'engaged' (Exodus 22:16-17), the severest penalty was not applied. According to Exodus 22:16-17 and Deuteronomy 22:28-29, the man had to either marry the woman or – if the father did not agree – pay a fine. Sexual relations between engaged couples is wrong, but it is not penalized. Sexual relations with someone to whom one is not engaged is viewed to be far worse.

---

[149] Compare this verse with Walter C. Kaiser. "The Weightier and Lighter Matters of the Law: Moses, Jesus and Paul." pp. 176-192 in: Gerald F. Hawthorne. Current Issues in Biblical and Patristic Studies: Studies in Honor of Merill C. Tenney. Wm. B. Eerdmans: Grand Rapids (MI), 1975; Comp. also the summary in Walter C. Kaiser. Towards Old Testament Ethics. Zondervan: Grand Rapids (MI), 1983. pp. 46-47. (Kaiser resolutely rejects, however, our view supported further below regarding ethical conflicts, ibid., p. 185, note 32).

3. Deciding Situationally

Example from the state sector

> *In public ethics it is also important not only to consider what is forbidden and what is to be punished by the state, but rather also how the bans relate to each other and how severe the respective penalties should be.* The state legal system is built on the idea that different offences are punished differently according to their severity. Even if we must be careful about indiscriminately transferring Old Testament law to our time and overlooking the changes from New Testament times, we still get some important tips for a just legal system. In the Old Testament the severity of the penalty is a way to recognize that offences against individuals (God or people) are significantly more severe than offences involving things. All offences in the Old Testament that carry the severest penalties are against God or against human life and human well-being. For that reason theft is less severely punished from the outset (never with death), as was generally the case in the Middle East or among Germanic peoples[150] with respect to grand larceny. "It is interesting to note that Ancient Near Eastern cuneiform law prescribes capital punishment for crimes against property, but in the Old Testament no crime against property warrants capital punishment. Once again, the point is that life is sacred, not things. Anything that aims at destroying the sacred quality of life is a capital offence against God."[151]

How to react against sin?

There are many biblical commands that describe for us how God originally thought about this world and how various areas of life looked before sin carried them away in its wake. This 'ideal' order is protected by commands. This applies, for instance, to marriage and the associated command that should protect it: "You shall not commit adultery."

With many biblical commands and in Christian ethics, the question is not about how the 'ideal' situation should look. *On the contrary, what is regulated is what has to happen if sin or mistakes have already occurred.* Acting in self-defense is an action that would not be allowed if there were not a sin that preceded it.

Example from the state sector

> An example is war. In a sinless world there would und should be no war. For that reason, it is always sin to start a war in peacetime (Hebrew: shalom). Insofar as this is concerned, pacifists are correct. They are incorrect, however,

---

[150] According to "Diebstahl." p. 549 in: Hellmut Brunner et al. (ed.). Lexikon Alter Kulturen. Vol. 1: A-Fir. Meyers Lexikonverlag: Mannheim, 1990.

[151] Walter C. Kaiser. Towards Old Testament Ethics. op. cit., p. 92.

if they conclude that in principal one is not allowed to react to acts of war or strife and unrighteousness with defense and war. Just war in the Bible is always a reaction to existing evil found in great measure.

Example from the family sector

The topic Divorce and Remarriage: of course both of these are unthinkable and superfluous in an 'ideal' situation. But they are both addressed in the Bible "because your hearts were hard" (Matthew 19:8; Mark 10:5). The Bible governs how one is to react to a weighty transgression (see Deuteronomy 24:1: "if ... then").

The Bible regulates life in the real world, and that means: life in a fallen, sinful world. Biblical-Christian ethics are not allowed to be idealistic, but rather their bias towards God's steadfast commands in God's fallen creation is meant to make order possible. Generally what applies here is what Paul referred to in his special attempt to deal with all sinners: "In that case you would have to leave this world" (1 Corinthians 5:10b).

3.2. To lead situationally means to be wise

Law and wisdom

The Bible not only has the *law* of God (in the narrower sense), which is primarily found in the five books of Moses, or Torah. Alongside this one finds that commands are explicitly formulated everywhere in the Bible.[152] The Bible also contains 'wisdom', which is first and foremost found in what is called wisdom literature,[153] but which is also found throughout the entire Bible.

In addition to the immediately valid and directly implementable commands one finds wisdom, which makes a correct decision dependent on the respective situation and can only act correctly if the involved individuals are known. Wisdom can be passed on in proverbs, parables, narratives

---

[152] The Old Testament contains, above all, the law, history books (called 'early prophets' by the Jews), the prophets (called 'latter prophets' by the Jews), and wisdom literature and poetry. Even when each part of the Old Testament has its own independent literary character, its literary elements can appear in other parts. In this way, one not only finds psalms and songs in the book of Psalms, but also in the Pentateuch, addresses given by prophets are handed down in the history books, and prophets quote laws.

[153] Regarding actual wisdom literature, this includes, above all, Proverbs, Ecclesiastes, Song of Songs, and Job and in addition, Psalms 1, 37, 49, 73, 78, 91, 128. These texts are of significance for biblical-Christian ethics.

3. Deciding Situationally 99

serving as examples, and object lessons that are only true in normal cases (e.g., Proverbs 15:1; 22:6) but do not necessarily have to happen. "Ethical topics account for a broad spectrum, such that in the older writings the impression could arise that wisdom first and foremost has to do with ethics."[154]

For the interpretation and application of wisdom literature and for that matter all biblical texts that seek to convey practical wisdom, there are several items to consider that arise from the essence of wisdom.[155] *The particular character of wisdom and wisdom literature are the educationally formulated words of advice for concrete situations.*

Biblical wisdom literature and poetry are not traced back to direct revelation, but rather they pass on worldly wisdom formulated poetically and educationally by men of God. This wisdom arose under the inspiration of God's Spirit and provides worldly wisdom from life experiences. "In the book of Proverbs it is predominantly emphasized that wisdom comes about as a quality of life through certain discipline and upbringing."[156]

While the law of God can be taught to a child (e.g., Deuteronomy 6:4-9), education in wisdom also already begins in childhood, requires a lengthy willingness to learn, practice, and experience. The fact that adultery is forbidden can be learned quickly and also known early so that it offers a firm life resource. How a mournful individual is to be addressed, however, or how one's own laziness is to be overcome or a dispute to be avoided cannot be answered in one sentence. Rather, it requires lifelong learning and maturity.

That wisdom literature is significantly directed toward education is expressed first and foremost in the fact that they are written in a captivating manner.[157] This applies above all to many proverbs, of which several have

---

[154] Helmut Weber. Allgemeine Moraltheologie: Ruf und Antwort: Styria: Graz, 1991. p. 48.

[155] Comp with a description of the character of wisdom literature in Walter C. Kaiser. Towards Old Testament Ethics. Zondervan: Grand Rapids (MI), 1983. pp. 64-66; William E. Mouser. Walking in Wisdom: Studying the Proverbs of Solomon. IVP: Downers Grove (IL), 1983; Michael Parson. "Understanding the Book of Proverbs." The Banner of Truth Nr. 303 (Dec. 1988): 7-9, 17; from a Catholic point of view: Helmut Weber. Allgemeine Moraltheologie. op. cit., p. 48-51; from a historico-critical point of view: Gerhard von Rad. Weisheit in Israel. Neukirchener Verlag: Neukirchen, 1985.³ p. 120-125 (and the entire book).

[156] Michael Parson. "Understanding the Book of Proverbs." op. cit., p. 9.

[157] Ted Hildebrandt. "Proverbial Strings: Cohesion in Proverbs 10". Grace Theological Journal 11 (1990) 2: 171-185 makes it clear the book of Proverbs does not only contain catchy subject matter, but in contrast to the widely held view that proverbs were mostly indiscriminately strung together, they follow a reasonable pedagogi-

found their way into our culture and today often are regarded as adages. An example is, "Whoever digs a pit may fall into it ..." (Ecclesiastes 10:8). Such proverbs are also found outside of the actual wisdom literature.

Proverbs in the Bible

Large portions of the book of Proverbs and Ecclesiastes consists of proverbs, e.g.,
- Ecclesiastes 10:8: "Whoever digs a pit may fall into it ..."
- Proverbs 17:12: "Better to meet a bear robbed of her cubs than a fool in his folly."
- Proverbs 22:13: "The sluggard says, 'There is a lion outside!' or, 'I will be murdered in the streets!'"
- Proverbs 22:8: "He who sows wickedness reaps trouble ..."
- Matthew 15:14: "Leave them; they are blind guides. If a blind man leads a blind man, both will fall into a pit."
- Acts 20:35: "'It is more blessed to give than to receive.'"
- 1 Corinthians 5:6: "Don't you know that a little yeast works through the whole batch of dough?"

Proverbs quoted in the Bible that are from the living environment
- Numbers 21:27: "That is why the poets say ... "
- 1 Samuel 24:14: "As the old saying goes, 'From evildoers come evil deeds.'"
- Ezekiel 16:44: "Everyone who quotes proverbs will quote this proverb about you: 'Like mother, like daughter.'"
- Luke 4:23: "Surely you will quote this proverb to me: 'Physician, heal yourself!'"
- John 4:37: "Thus the saying 'One sows and another reaps' is true."
- 2 Peter 2:22: "Of them the proverbs are true: 'A dog returns to its vomit,' and, 'A sow that is washed goes back to her wallowing in the mud.'"

The 'situational ethics' of wisdom

Wisdom primarily provides general advice, which can only be put into practice in specific situations. In a completely different situation, their use would bring about precisely the opposite.

What we are dealing with here is a healthy 'situational ethic.' If situational ethics recognize God's commands and limits itself to situations that

---

cal layout; comp. also with William E. Mouser. Walking in Wisdom: Studying the Proverbs of Solomon. op. cit.

3. Deciding Situationally

are not clearly regulated by God's mandates, situational ethics "with biblical wisdom" can be an important supplement and a daily component of ethical decisions.[158]

A classic example for this is seen in Proverbs 26:4-5: "Do not answer a fool according to his folly, or you will be like him yourself. Answer a fool according to his folly, or he will be wise in his own eyes." Should a person answer a fool or not? The answer has two sides that have to be weighed according to the situation. The question of whether an individual should answer a fool and enter into his line of thinking or not is not decided once and for all by a command from God. The wise person has to decide in each case what he might achieve with a response to such an individual given a concrete situation.

A good example of a wise command that can be used in a concrete situation is found in texts that take into account that every individual can get tired of honey at some point: "If you find honey, eat just enough – too much of it, and you will vomit. Seldom set foot in your friends house – too much of you, and he will hate you" (Proverbs 25:16-17). "It is not good to eat too much honey, nor is it honorable to seek one's own honor" (Proverbs 25:27). At this point a general guideline is provided that can prevent much annoyance on both sides. How often a person should visit a good friend or how often a person should be praised cannot be communicated by a teacher of wisdom. What is required is a good understanding of the friend and a lot of life experience. To visit a good friend too often and to praise someone too much is indeed not a sin, but it is unwise and can lead to the end of a friendship.

It doesn't work without advice

In wisdom one finds that advice plays an important role. While the law is clear, and proper judges can watch over its compliance, and while the teacher of the law has the immediate authority of the law on his side, wisdom has to weigh numerous possibilities, bring together numerous experiences, and consider much advice.

In contrast to the proverb that 'too many cooks spoil the broth,' consultation and advice have a position of great importance in biblical wisdom literature. This applies first of all at a very basic level: "Plans fail for lack of counsel, but with many advisers they succeed" (Proverbs 15:22). This is even more the case where there is a lot of responsibility: "For lack of guid-

---

[158] This is demonstrated particularly well in James I. Packer. "Situations and Principles." pp. 148-156 in: David K. Clark, Robert V. Rakestraw. Readings in Christian Ethics. Vol. 1: Theory and Method. Baker Books: Grand Rapids, 1994.

ance a nation falls, but many advisers make victory sure" (Proverbs 11:14). With advice there is no teacher of the law who gives a final answer (even if the law provides a framework for all decisions that cannot be abandoned). Rather, wise individuals give their grounds for why they hold one way to be better than another. What is in view is above all the result of actions and decisions.

To look for, apply, test, recognize, learn, ask, listen, become wise, advise as well as similar notions in the Bible all describe in repeatedly new twists and turns the way to make the wisest decision. We have just seen in the case of self control that a God-fearing individual does not just start talking away and doing things. Rather, he calmly and soberly considers the consequences of his decisions.

While the teacher of the law knows the entire law and can communicate it, the wise individual can only pass on what he has personally learned. Proverbs 11:2b reads as follows: "… with humility comes wisdom." Humility is noticeable in the fact that it willingly calls upon others with whom to consult, considers their judgment, and does not consider oneself to be omniscient.

Example from family life

> A married couple calls on me and wants to know whether they should have any more children. Both are employed and pay to support children from first marriages who live with the prior marriage partners who do not work. The income the married couple has is barely enough to cover living costs, much less pay for their own children. And yet the desire to have children is present in both of them. Their situation is everything other than ideal. As a pastor I have to pay attention to the fact that they have confessed their guilt before God and among people and have received forgiveness. Even if basic biblical values regarding marriage and family, work, and much else play an important role, the question the couple have cannot be answered in an absolute manner. What is sought in a pastoral conversation is guidance, a discussion of unconventional solutions and information about who else might be able to offer advice. Questions regarding the situation in the new marriage, problems encountered in raising the existing children and their attitudes towards money and possessions might also arise. It will also be mentioned that money is not everything and that one often simply has to trust God – not as a patent recipe or command, but rather due to the fact that trust in God belongs in every wise decision. Still, in the final event, none of this can answer the question. Rather, it can only offer assistance so that the married couple can make their own wise decision, for which they will be responsible and behind which they must stand.

3. Deciding Situationally

Example from church life

In pastoral care there are always two aspects: On the one hand, the pastor has to know God's commands and hold them up as a mirror before a fellow Christian. This can serve either to encourage the Christian to keep God's laws, or to call upon him to ask for forgiveness of his sin and to repent. On the other hand, there can be problems which have nothing to do with keeping or breaking God's commands but rather are cases where wise decisions are required. At this point the pastor can refer to wisdom texts in the Bible, refer to his own experiences, offer advice, and can lead the individual to consider the consequences of his actions. With this, however, he does not have the same authority as when he is able to invoke God's word.

Example from the state sector

A parliament does not only exist because there is otherwise no practical way to represent a people when explicit decisions have to be made. In fact, a parliament expresses the conviction that broad discussion and consultation about specific questions and situations bring about the best result. When the German Parliament has a decision to make about how the public is to be protected from, say, attack dogs, that presupposes a comprehensive inquiry of the entire situation that makes it possible for other opinions to be voiced and discussed other than just that of the individual injured by the attack dog. The situation (people assailed by an attack dog) evokes the question: How can individuals (particularly children and the elderly) be protected from attack dogs? Every new situation requires sensible measures. Normative thought and entering into the specific situation have to go hand in hand.

Example from the business sector

A businessman considers whether it is a good idea to put his company into his son's hands and if so, how. As a person well aware of the Bible's contents, he knows that God has so fashioned the creation that younger generations finally take over and that older generations retain advisory positions. He also realizes, however, that there is a responsibility towards his employees and fears that his son might possibly split up the company, selling off the more lucrative parts. On the other hand, the less successful parts might 'go to the dogs,' since their profits are less than the interest received on a time deposit. For the elderly boss, the profit was enough to justify keeping the company, but from the standpoint of other investors this does not play a role. When and how should the takeover occur? In addition to the several basic values (profit is not everything; keeping jobs in place, obligations towards longtime employees, loyalty to the location where the company is situated also counts) there are chiefly innumerable interests to be balanced and many details relating to the situation that play a role. No one can expect a quick and unruffled answer, and any expert advice is welcome. Numerous possible combinations and interim solutions will surely be compiled. Finally, after considering all the normative and situational values, the decision will be an existential one, which the businessman 'will make on his own' (as a Christian communicating with God) and for which consequences he will have to be responsible. The decision that came after two and one-half years made the best of the situation: The son takes over the lucrative part of the business under the condition, confirmed by a notary, to leave the main plant at the present location for a period of ten years. The other parts of the company will be spun off as a limited liability company. The employees will be able to become shareholders, and initially the businessman will continue to run the limited liability company as the chief executive until an employee is able to take over the tasks.

How can this be conveyed to a secular environment?
Whoever allows only the current situation to be considered in a decision can simply decide and justify anything or nothing. Whoever only accepts values and prescribed boundaries is not in a position to put these appropriately into practice. The art consists in implementing and translating the given (current or long term) unchanging values in ever new (and in part also 'impossible') situations.

The results of our actions

Above all, wisdom argues from the standpoint of the results of actions taken.

"In wisdom's view, what to do and what not to do are both derived from actions taken and, more precisely, from their consequences. It is a matter of the consequences that are attached to the individual actions that make them appear either advisable or inadvisable."[159]

Above all, teachers of wisdom know these consequences via their experiences, that is to say, through observation of their own life and the lives of others. They reckon that every individual who has had these experiences can understand and confirm their observations. "The most striking characteristic of the wisdom ethos is the way in which it is presented. It occurs – other than in the law and with the prophets – almost exclusively without the proclamation of direct demands or prohibitions, but rather by conveying insights and experiences. It is not an ethos of commands. Rather, it is a morality has to do with advice and arguments from reason."[160] "A further characteristic of the wisdom ethos is, then, its orientation towards succeed-

---

[159] Helmut Weber. Allgemeine Moraltheologie. op. cit., p. 49.
[160] Ibid.

ing in human life. The goal is as happy and harmonious a life as possible."[161]

Hendrik van Oyen formulates it similarly: "This single normative authority is the creation-like expression of order and being in the world, which constantly makes itself noticeable as a fact of experience and unavoidably matches our action and the tab it leaves."[162]

Such it is that in the book of Proverbs "sin" (Hebrew *paesa*) is used twelve times, but never directly is sin against God mentioned.[163] From this one may not conclude that wisdom expresses purely human considerations, while the law proclaims divine, revealed commands. Wisdom presupposes faith in a God who reveals himself and views this as God's word.

For the teachers of wisdom there are various justifications for things.[164] In many Proverbs, the second part of the sentence begins with "for," whereby various explanatory statements are given, revealing paradigmatic consequences that can extend all the way up to God's judgment. It is often the case that other respective grounds could have been given. The reasons are not basic and unique, but rather they are chosen on the basis of pedagogical-practical principles."[165]

Arguments from future consequences in Proverbs 22-27 (examples)

- Proverbs 22:25: (against associating with hot-tempered individuals) "... or you may learn his ways and get yourself ensnared."
- Proverbs 22:27: (against pledges and guarantees:) "... if you lack the means to pay, your very bed will be snatched from under you."
- Proverbs 23:11: (against deceiving the fatherless:) "... for their Defender is strong; he will take up their case against you."
- Proverbs 23:21: (against gluttony:) "for drunkards and gluttons become poor, and drowsiness clothes them in rags."
- Proverbs 24:12: (against concealment:) "... does not he who weighs the heart perceive it? Does not he who guards your life know it? Will he not repay each person according to what he has done?"
- Proverbs 24:16: "... for though a righteous man falls seven times, he rises again, but the wicked are brought down by calamity."

---

[161] Ibid.

[162] Hendrik van Oyen. Ethik des Alten Testaments. Gütersloher Verlagshaus Gerd Mohn: Gütersloh, 1967. p. 143.

[163] According to Gerhard von Rad. Weisheit in Israel. op. cit., p. 120.

[164] Cf. Gerhard von Rad. Weisheit in Israel. op. cit., pp.. 120-124.

[165] Ibid., p. 122.

- Proverbs 24:18: (against Schadenfreude, pleasure gained from the misfortune of others) "... or the LORD will see and disapprove and turn his wrath away from him."
- Proverbs 24:22: (warning against rebels) "... for those two will send sudden destruction upon them."
- Proverbs 25:8: "... do not bring hastily to court, for what will you do in the end if your neighbor puts you to shame?"
- Proverbs 25:17: "... too much of you, and he will hate you."
- Proverbs 27:1: "Do not boast about tomorrow, for you do not know what a day may bring forth."
- Proverbs 27:24: "... for riches do not endure forever ..."

Regarding 'consequentialism'

The preceding list of pieces of wisdom should not be understood as a case for 'consequentialism,' which is certainly the most widespread ethical theory of our time in secular as well as Christian circles. It involves individuals' deciding solely based on consequences and on future probability, not, however, on the basis of values that currently define good and evil completely independent of future developments. The end (future consequence) thereby justifies the mean.[166]

The former Pope spoke of "theological ethics (proportionalism, consequentialism)," which teach that "an absolute normative enjoinder can never be formulated."[167]

The following can be said regarding consequentialism:
1. Consequentialism contradicts clear biblical declarations, not the least of which is Romans 3:8: "Why not say – as we are being slanderously reported as saying and as some claim that we say – 'Let us do evil that

---

[166] For a critique comp. with a philosophical point of view Robert Spaemann. "Die schlechte Lehre vom guten Zweck." Frankfurter Allgemeine Zeitung Nr. 247 dated October 23, 1999, Supplement 'Bilder und Zeiten,' pp. I-II, reprinted in Leben: Das CDL-Info 1/2000: 21-25; Julian Nida-Rümelin. Kritik des Konsequentialismus. R. Oldenbourg: München, 1993^1 (1995^2) und Elisabeth Anscombe. "Statt einer Einführung." pp. 3-9 in: Julian Nida-Rümelin. Kritik des Konsequentialismus. op. cit., Reprint of the article "Modern Moral Philosophy" from 1958 (printouts ibid. notes *) (Anscombe coined the term "consequentialism" in 1958); from the theological point of view John Paul II. Encyclical Veritatis splendor. August 6, 1993. Verlautbarungen des Apostolischen Stuhls 111. Sekretariat der Deutschen Bischofskonferenz: Bonn, 1995^5 (1993^1). pp. 70-81 (Kap. IV "Die sittliche Handlung").

[167] Ibid., p. 74.

good may result'? Their condemnation is deserved." The intention a person has also plays an important role in the Bible (comp. the evil intentions of the Pharisees in Mark 7:20-21; Matthew 15:19). The intention is a) only one ethical criterion among others and not the sole criterion, and b) an evil act does not become good with good intentions, that is to say, that a robbery homicide does not become good if the criminal robs the individual and desires to give the money to a good cause.[168]
2. In consequentialism individuals are given an "excessive responsibility,"[169] because they are made responsible for the consequences that they can either influence only slightly or not at all.
3. In consequentialism individuals have to incessantly be prophets. In reality an individual can often only estimate and vaguely discern what the consequences might be, but "an exhaustively reasonable calculation is not possible."[170] One always knows more in hindsight.
4. Finally, in consequentialism everything can be explained by the fact of the 'lesser evil,' that is to say, that everything could have been even worse.[171] The doctor at the concentration camp, who remains because another doctor in his place would have killed even more people, acts as morally as a politician who approves a poison gas production facility because jobs are thereby maintained.
5. Such examples show that also in the case of consequentialism the question of the priority of values does not pass away. How many jobs does it take to outweigh the dangers of poison gas? Can adultery be justified by the fact that in the act a depressive person is thereby made happy? Or what weight does 'making someone happy' have over against other values?

Pope John Paul II noted correctly that Christian ethics by all means incorporates the consequences of actions taken, however not in an absolute sense and not in order to annul the clear commands found within Christian ethics. There is, then, a difference between a situation where consequences

---

[168] Particularly ibid., pp. 71, 76.
[169] Elisabeth Anscombe. "Statt einer Einführung." op. cit., pp. 90-92 (section title).
[170] John Paul II. Encyclical Veritatis splendor. op. cit., p. 77, see the justification pp. 76-77.
[171] Particularly according to Elisabeth Anscombe. "Statt einer Einführung." op. cit., p. 92-94.

can be estimated in a particular case and a question that can be clearly answered ethically.[172]

Christian ethics insistently consider the consequences of our actions, but they do not raise them to be an absolute principle. Rather, they integrate them into a normative framework and overall situation.

4. Deciding existentially

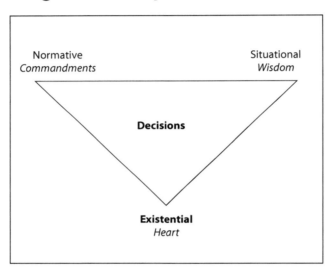

4.1. Leading existentially means internalizing what one does

With respect to God, what a person does is never a question of simple external fulfillment of his commands, but rather pursuing positive values out of internal conviction and love. The Apostle Paul formulated this tellingly: "The goal of this command is love, which comes from a pure heart and a good conscience and a sincere faith" (1 Timothy 1:5).

Values are always internal values, even when they are expressed externally. Surely it is better that the state's laws prevent me from murdering rather than giving physical expression to my 'internal desire to commit murder.' However, the goal of the prohibition of murder is not solely to

---

[172] John Paul II. Encyclical Veritatis splendor. op. cit., p. 76. The Pope naturally refers to Biblical commands as well as to all other commands proclaimed by the papal teaching office.

prevent a murder but to overcome internal hatred with love. For this reason Paul writes to the Roman Christians that many people only obey the state out of fear of punishment (Romans 13:1-5). Christians on the contrary should do what is stipulated to be good "not only because of possible punishment but also because of conscience" (Romans 13:5).

How can this be conveyed to a secular environment?
For an individual's own decision, as well as for everyone who is affected by the decision, it is important that the normative and situational elements come together to yield a decision about which we are in inwardly convinced. To be sure, internal approval should not be raised to a level of dogma and seen as the sole criterion. Sometimes the decision maker has to decide quickly and matter-of-factly without waiting long enough to find 'comfort' with the situation. And an individual cannot always wait until all the parties involved appreciate the sense of a decision. But whoever continually passes over his and others most deeply held internal convictions, always leaves involved parties in the dark, and does not attempt to get their understanding and approval, is asking too much of himself and his colleagues.

The internal attitude in the Old Testament

It can be recognized in the Old Testament that God is not solely concerned with the external fulfillment of commands. Some Christians are of the opinion that in Matthew 5:27-32 Jesus added to the 'external' command against adultery by giving an 'internal' command against lustful looks. In reality, however, the command against adultery is already found in the Ten Commandments as is the command against lust: "You shall not covet your neighbor's wife ..." (Exodus 20:17).[173] This tenth commandment presents the internal side of the command against adultery (coveting a neighbor's wife) and of the command against theft. Wrongly coveting is repeatedly condemned in the Old Testament.[174] The book of Proverbs concerns itself with the grievous and destructive yearning for another woman. In Job 31:1 we read in this connection: "I made a covenant with my eyes not to look

---

[173] Klaus Bockmühl. Christliche Lebensführung: Eine Ethik der Zehn Gebote. TVG. Brunnen: Gießen, 1993. p. 146. I value Klaus Bockmühl's work but why he writes that Jesus 'radicalized' the tenth commandment is not clear to me. Which case is forbidden by Jesus that was not already forbidden by in the Old Testament?

[174] Comp. Alexander Rofé. "The Tenth Commandment in the Light of Four Deuteronomic Laws." pp. 45-66 in: Ben-Zion Segal, Gershon Levi (Hg.). The Ten Commandments in History and Tradition. The Magnes Press (The Hebrew University): Jerusalem, 1990.

lustfully at a girl." According to Numbers 15:39, Israel should always be reminded of the law: "... so you will remember all the commands of the Lord, that you may obey them and not prostitute yourselves by going after the lusts of your own hearts and eyes." Proverbs 6:25 also warns against the adulteress: "Do not lust in your heart after her beauty or let her captivate you with her eyes ..."

Many commentators think that in Matthew 5:21-26 Jesus actually sharpens and internalizes the command against murder by forbidding baseless anger towards another expressed in swear words. After all, the one-sided interpretation of the Old Testament law that only looks at an action was one of the errors of the teachers of the law. The Old Testament itself clearly differentiated between sin and the planning of sin. And just as clearly as the New Testament, the Old Testament condemns the evil planning of sin. Whoever wishes to serve God has to do this with his entire heart.[175] Just as internal desire provokes, for example, adultery, so does uncontrolled anger lead to murder. Anger plots murder (Esther 5:9), is cruel (Proverbs 27:4), and mauls others (Amos 1:11). Men are slain in anger (Genesis 49:6-7; Deuteronomy 19:6) and "a king's wrath is a messenger of death" (Proverbs 16:14), to name just a few passages in the Old Testament. "Old Testament ethics are as much concerned with the *internal* response to Old Testament morality as to the outward acts."[176] Evil thoughts are repeatedly addressed and condemned by God (e.g., Genesis 6:5; 1 Chronicles 28:9; Proverbs 6:16-18; 15:26; 21:27; Isaiah 59:7; Jeremiah 4:14; Ezekiel 38:10; Psalm 94:11).

Example from church life

> Paul's command to not make membership in the church dependent on "passing judgment on disputable matters" (Romans 14:1), and Paul's demand that the 'strong in the faith' respect those who are 'weak in the faith,' reminds us that the Church of Jesus Christ has to differentiate between unambiguous commands from God and such traditions that may be sensible but never, however, can be made compulsory for everyone. This view that Paul had was one of the major discoveries of the Reformation! With respect to disputable questions in the church in Rome (respecting certain holidays and eating meat used in sacrifices), it is completely clear which position Paul supports. For him God has neither forbidden meat nor wine nor has he made certain holidays a rule for everyone. That Paul makes his position known so clearly is all the more astounding in that he directs his exhortation to the strong and

---

[175] See particularly also Walter C. Kaiser. Toward Rediscovering the Old Testament. Zondervan: Grand Rapids (MI), 1987. pp. 128-133.

[176] Walter C. Kaiser. Towards Old Testament Ethics. op. cit., p. 7.

4. Deciding existentially

seeks to provide protection for the weak. In 1 Corinthians 10:22-33 Paul states his position even more clearly. Why, then, does he not want to see his position put into practice, which is expressed when he says, "... and everything that does not come from faith is sin" (Romans 14:23)? Under "faith" in Romans 14:23, as in the preceding context, the conviction to be understood is that God has permitted something.[177] It is not general faith in God that is intended at this point. Paul explains to those who want to put pressure on individuals who are "weak in the faith" that not everything is achieved if the weak externally comply. Those who are "weak in the faith" do not have to be at the liberty of the "strong in the faith," nor do they have to consciously act as if they know they are doing something against the will of God. Rather, they should do what they do in the knowledge and trust that God has allowed it. Paul apparently wants the weak to eat meat associated with sacrifices only if they are convinced that they as Christians are allowed to partake in such a meal. He does not want Christians to act against their inner convictions or to only conform externally. Rather, Paul wants Christians to act out of conscious conviction and out of faith that what they are doing has not been forbidden by God.

Example from the business sector

When talking about the work ethic, the internal attitude of a person is very important. I can set up many rules relating to the workplace and exert significant control over employees, but that is not a cure for an inner resistance to work. An inner refusal can only be overcome if I address the blocks and relationship problems that are at its root (e.g., perpetual contention with a department head or covert drinking at home) or by at least achieving a minimum of inner consent towards work, the company, and the management style.

Example from family life

When my father was awarded the Federal Republic of Germany's Order of Merit on his eightieth birthday, I held a short laudatory speech on behalf of the family. The assembled political notables (as far as I know not practicing Christians) were not lightly astonished when I mentioned that my parents had raised us to be 'world citizens' and that thanks to my upbringing I could not emotionally comprehend hate towards foreigners or disdain for the disabled. How did my parents do it? When we were growing up, we occasionally talked about such topics. Sometimes comments were made about what a

---

[177] Also C. E. B. Cranfield. A Critical and Exegetical Commentary on The Epistle to the Romans. 2 Vols. The International Critical Commentary 11. T & T Clark: Edinburgh, 1989 (1979 revised reprint). Vol. 2., pp. 728-729, who before presents and discusses various interpretations of Romans 14:23.

newspaper said about such subject matter. However, the actual way opposition to hatred toward foreigners was impressed upon us was the way my parents placed a high value on love towards all people and practiced this attitude. Therefore, at our home we got to know many people from all over the world (not on television or via derogatory jokes) and saw how our parents respected and valued them. That I, as a small child, was allowed to rub the hair of an African, who afterwards gave a fascinating lecture as a world leader, was something that conspicuously communicated to me that he was a person just like I am, and that he was someone who needed trust and was someone for whom my respect was valuable.

Example from the state sector

The basic values of a society cannot arise merely from societal consensus. We can even ask ourselves if common convictions still rule in our society. If agreement alone is what counts, then National Socialism would have had to be accepted as long as it could have held the enthusiastic approval of large parts of the population. It was precisely due to the lesson learned from the time of National Socialism that there had to be inviolable values beyond the jurisdiction of a state. For this reason the United Nations created The Universal Declaration of Human Rights, and for this reason the composers of the German Constitution established several basic rights relating to human dignity, which may not be deleted from the constitution. Human rights and human dignity are not created by the state nor are they awarded by the state. Rather, they are given by the fact that man is created by God. This is an inviolable arrangement that is apparent to all people and stands above all authority and any majority. Nevertheless, the following applies: *On the one hand, the basic values of a society have to be inviolable and stand outside and above themselves, and simultaneously they have to meet with the agreement of at least a large portion of the population.* Over the long term, no society can have completely different values and rights in its constitution and legal structure from those it practices and which are at least theoretically accepted by a significant portion of the population. The caste system in India was abolished by the Constitution after World War II, but up until today it still determines public life in spite of all the indications of progress. This is due to the fact that the majority of Indians remain captive to the caste system in their thinking and acting.

4.2. Leading existentially means gaining experience

An apparently difficult topic is how to interlace the study of the Holy Scriptures with insights gained by tradition, experience, and sensible deliberation which we discussed in chapter 2.1. As basically correct as the desire is to not wish to read the Bible through the glasses of our own world view, it is unavoidable that my biography codetermines my Bible reading. What is important is a continual interplay, in which the Holy Scriptures play the normative role while the personality of the reader also plays a meaningful role. The Bible calls for changes that God's Holy Spirit seeks to effect in us. At the same time, these changes, however, lead us to read the Holy Scriptures in another light and open up new aspects.

Whoever begins as a child to read the Bible reads God's word, albeit through the glasses of a child. As one's personality matures, so does one's understanding of the Bible. With new experiences new parts of the Bible, which were also parts of God's word but had little to do with one's personal life or doctrine, also become understandable. Personally experienced suffering can, for instance, open up the Psalms of lament, the book of the prophet Jeremiah, Lamentations or the book of Job in ways never known before. Our presuppositions and the horizon provided by our experiences are indispensible, even when the Bible continually changes and determines our experiential horizon.

God often leads people step by step out of false traditions and uses concrete experience as well as normative aspects.

Example from church life

> The Apostles learned via the interplay of direct revelation, the study of the Old Testament, and personal experience that Jesus' church was going to be drawn from all peoples and was no longer solely bound to the Jewish people. The book of Acts is an eloquent testimony to this. What was it that brought the Apostle Peter to this new conviction? Jesus' teaching, the visions of the "unclean" animals (Acts 10:9-20), the profoundly impressive experience of Cornelius' conversion (Acts 10:24ff) and other pagans, discussions with Paul (Galatians 2:11ff) and others, or the dictates of the events, for instance, by which pagans in Antioch were converted (Acts 11:1-18) without asking for permission in Jerusalem? Everything together convinced Peter, as the Council at Jerusalem indicates. His primary argument is personal experience (Acts 15:7-9; comp. 15:14); it is likewise with Paul and Barnabas: Acts 15:12), even if the consent of the Holy Spirit tipped the scales (Acts 15:15-19). Purely theoretically it would have been best if the Apostles had studied the Bible, understood it, and put it into practice. Reality was something else, however, because the Apostles were also just men of flesh and blood and not computers which could be reprogrammed with new software. Christ's disciples hesitated to implement the Great Commission, not because they had not been given it, but rather because it had not yet been connected with their experience and therefore had not yet affected their hearts.

4.3. To existentially lead means to suffer vicariously and to cultivate relationships

At this point we have to repeat much of what we initially said about love. If our decisions are determined by love, then they also have something to do with relationships. Even for one or the other difficult decisions, I am not able to withdraw myself from the relational aspect. My 'suffering with' others is still called for.

In our universe everything ultimately has a personal and ethical nature, and everything that is decided upon happens with respect to relationships between individuals. Biblical ethics is for that reason always personal ethics. In the final event everything always has to do with the relationship of people to each other, as the Ten Commandments, for instance, make clear. At the same time, this also establishes the integrated nature of biblical ethics, which do not stop at individual factual issues. Rather, biblical ethics looks at everything together, at the relationship level between God and man as well as the relationships that individuals have with each other.

Management decisions can never ignore the fact that they are always made in a way that affects relationships between people and possibly even decides their fate. This does not mean that one cannot and may not decide factually and level-headedly. But it does mean that the consequences that a decision has for other people, and the meaning that this decision has for the relationship to subordinates and among subordinates, is a significant factor in the evaluation of interests.

How can this be conveyed to a secular environment?
Knowledge, experience, maturity, and character building all have to be equally taken into account with the choice of executives. It is not only IQ that counts. The emotional quotient (EQ), also called 'emotional intelligence,' is also important.[178]

---

[178] Comp. Daniel Goleman. Emotionale Intelligenz. Hanser: München, 1996 same as dtv: München, 1997; Robert K. Cooper, Ayman Sawaf. Emotionale Intelligenz für Manager. Heyne: München, 1997; Branko Bokun. Wer lacht lebt. Ariston: München, 1996; Andreas Huber. Stichwort Emotionale Intelligenz. Heyne: München, 1996.⁴ In 1962, at the famous Ciba Symposium regarding the future of humanity, the overestimation of IQ and the importance of having the ability to get along with other people was pointed out [Robert Jungk, Hans Josef Mundt (ed.).] Das Umstrittene Experiment: Der Mensch. Siebenundzwanzig Wissenschaftler diskutieren die Elemente einer biologischen Revolution. Kurt Desch: München, 1966. p. 304 [English original Gordon Wolstenhom (ed.). Man and His Future. J. & A. Churchill: London, 1963].

In the following we want to limit ourselves to examples having to do with the state and the business world, because the importance of cultivating relationships for responsible parties in families is clear to everyone. It has to be made clear that a business person can no less forgo investing work, time, money, and thought into relationships than, for instance, a mother or a pastor in their respective environments.

General example

> Helmut Kohl was a leading politician of his time. And it is well established what a large role Helmut Kohl's long term personal relationships played in German reunification. In connection with that historical even, trust was placed in the idea that the Germans were not seeking to uncouple themselves from the Western alliance. There was also trust in the idea that Germans were not entertaining any revenge towards the previous Soviet Union or that they were seeking to amend being displaced from earlier areas that now belonged to the East. This trust was not significantly due to trust in the German people, but rather it was due to trust in the reliability of one person who credibly represented the German people. In this connection, there was a celebrated meeting held between Helmut Kohl and Mikhail Gorbachev in Caucasus. During that meeting Helmut Kohl acquired Gorbachev's approval for Germany to remain a member of NATO, while Gorbachev in turn received Kohl's promise that an honorable and financially supported withdrawal of Soviet troops from the prior German Democratic Republic would take place. This would have all been unthinkable if the relationship between the two statesmen going into the meeting had not been preceded by a period during which a relationship of trust had been cultivated.

General example

> Think of a successful company owner who makes savvy decisions and puts his company on a growth path. However, at the same time he demonstrates no personal interest in his managers, not to mention his other employees. Not only is such a businessman a humanly disagreeable boss, his is also not someone who really thinks strategically. Think of how quickly a situation could arise where he is dependent on the goodwill of his employees! If orders fall off; if the company encounters difficulties and everyone has to suffer the loss; if he suddenly is suspected of tax fraud or becomes gravely ill, the survival of the company could very well depend on the trust his employees have in him. At that point it will be demonstrated whether they are ready to put themselves on the line for him and for his company, or whether they all 'have an outstanding score' with him.

General example

> Laying off an employee can indeed be done in love, if an individual, for example, would otherwise be completely out of his or her depth. It could also be out of love towards all the remaining employees of the organization, whose jobs would thereby be more assured. Still, whoever lets go of employees out of love will take time to tell the involved party the reasons for the termination (showing, for instance, the collision of duties), so that the involved party might better understand what this hard decision means for him or her. Whoever, on the other hand, dismisses employees as an act of revenge, selfishness, harassment, or touchiness about criticism will shy away from meeting face to face with the involved party. The decision maker will hide behind a letter or barricade himself behind the authority of his position.

How can this be conveyed to a secular environment?

We have already pointed out the example of building a house. A good architect may know everything about building a house and win every court case against the authorities and construction companies. If, however, he is not interested in the essence of what he does, namely the individual or individuals who live in the houses he designs, in the end he will remain a bad architect because he has no idea why he is building anything. This is due to the fact that a house, no matter how beautiful it might be, is of no consequence. His buildings will pass by the lives for which they were intended. Houses are constructed for people. People are not born for houses. What Jesus once said about the Sabbath ("The Sabbath was made for man, not man for the Sabbath," Mark 2:27) applies to all areas of creation. It applies to work, business, and management structures. People do not exist in order to fulfill these structures, but rather all these structures were created for the benefit of people. Whenever we forget that we live and work for people and not for robots or for profit maximization, we will live and work *against* people knowingly or unknowingly. And in the end that will not only destroy people, but rather also everything that people produce.

Example from the business sector

> An unhappy worker is also a poor worker, and a halfhearted manager will probably make bad decisions. A customer who is treated impolitely and is irritated is in the best case an aggravated customer and in the worst case lodges complaints and is a future 'non-customer.' Every bit of cooperative work and economic activity presuppose a minimum of agreement and trust. When these factors are destroyed, economic activity at most becomes thinkable as slavery or a mafia-like structure. Whoever invests in relationships invests at the same time in the most important capital a company has, a person who can only truly work well if he works in good association with others.

4.4. To lead existentially means to simultaneously indict and defend

The Lord of the universe, Jesus Christ, is the perfect judge, because he takes charges seriously but at the same time is the defender of those who believe in him.

The mixture of healthy accusation and self-evident defense is what determines true authority in all areas of life. We can own up to someone who 'indicts' and accuses us if at the same time that person is an advocate. For that reason a good marriage, for example, can favorably accept massive criticism given by someone in private and find such to be of help, which outside of the marriage would be seen as character assassination.

How can this be conveyed to a secular environment?
True authority comes via a complementarity between form and freedom, between inflexibility and flexibility, between leading and allowing independent decisions. Where boundaries or form is emphasized and freedom is crushed, rigidity, coercion and tyranny arise. Where freedom overwhelms borders, weakness, indifference, and anarchy arise. True authority is consequential but not callous, flexible but not without boundaries. True authority is a simultaneous balance of consistency and flexibility. Neither the tyrant nor the 'wimp,' neither the 'howler monkey' nor the pussyfooter, neither the person who decides everything on his own nor the individual who cannot make decisions, is an ideal of Christian authority and leadership.

Example from family life

> Good parents bring their children via criticism and punishment, but also via unselfish acceptance and unconditional advocacy, to a healthy self-assessment. Whoever is truly there for his children will teach them a healthy self-criticism by setting disclosing boundaries for his children as well as a healthy self-confidence by defending and forgiving his children. I can vividly remember how my brother once smashed the neighbors' window with a soccer ball. My father did three things: 1. He scolded and set a punishment (the learning effect: carelessness can do damage to others). 2. He explained to my brother how things like this happen and how he could avoid this mistake in the future, whereby he recounted an example from his own youth (learning effect: a) there are always reasons for exoneration, even when these do not eliminate guilt, b) it makes sense to sound out the reasons for the mistake in order to avoid it the next time; c) every person makes mistakes – my self-assessment does not rest on my flawlessness). 3. He went to the neighbor and explained what was for us unforgettable – "*We* broke your

window and we want to pay to replace it!" My father was not only the accuser and judge, he was also the one who as defender brought arguments of exoneration and who to the outside did not come before his children and say, "Unfortunately I have such a bad son; I just don't know where that came from!"

Example from pastoral life

A pastor who only tells his counselee what he or she wants to hear, is just as unhelpful as one who has only one goal: to uncover another's sins and await a confession. A pastor can have the function of accuser, if he holds up a mirror to the counselee and takes away the veil of self-deception. But the prophet Nathan changed direction when David realized his guilt; then Nathan spoke about forgiveness. A pastor can also have the other function of a defender, if a bad conscience is plaguing the counselee with something that is not true guilt. Sexually abused children must be told that the guilt does not rest with them but with the adults, although children often are tormented by the thought that they are themselves guilty. At this point the pastor becomes the one who absolves. A pastor needs both: the courage to call a spade a spade, and to vocalize charges ("Actually they really do not want to!") as well as the courage to suffer vicariously and to be an advocate, to forgive him, and to make it clear to him that many individuals have this problem. The pastor is at one's disposal, as it were, for an objective parley about problems, in which all the incriminating evidence as well as all the exonerating evidence is put on the table. The pastor is of course not the judge who pronounces a judgment. If he did so, he would place himself in God's position. He only helps to make a good decision, something that we as people often cannot do alone.

Example from the state sector

A good legal system ensures that both charges as well as defense work and that neither can be hindered. It is the state that stands up for law and punishment – this is why the state provides a district attorney. The state also stands against injustice and excessive penalties. It is for this reason that the state assists in defense and even, in the case of the weak, provides relief for the costs arising in court proceedings by paying for the defense or assigning counsel. A well organized defense and a poorly prepared prosecution (e.g., via underpaid police and district attorney, too few personnel, bureaucratic restrictions and corruption) can too easily lead to injustice in the same way that a well organized prosecution does in the face of a poor defense (e.g., via a lack of financial resources, obstruction, a lack of knowledge, and threats).

4. Deciding existentially 119

Example: the social security net

A similar situation applies to the social security net. The state has to ensure that the socially weak are not 'excluded' and at the same time that they do not wrongly take advantage of services. The state, then, comes out as a defender of the socially weak and simultaneously as the accuser over against those who abuse these services.

Example: a worker works less

Let us look at an example where a good employee who works in the production of industrial tents is known for his reliable work. For weeks a number of complaints from customers has been accumulating because rain comes in through the tents. The owner of this mid-sized company has to confront his employees. How can he proceed without breaking too much china?

1. He gives the involved party an opportunity to describe his view of things or to offer an apology.
2. First of all he thanks the involved person for his long years of reliable work.
3. He informs himself in advance of what might possibly be the cause of the drop in excellence. In the course of his investigation his suspicion is confirmed. The employee's daughter has been in the hospital for weeks in a life and death condition, caused by a traffic accident for which her father is responsible.

If the employee notices that the boss does not first come as a prosecutor but rather simultaneously as a defender who knows the reasons for exoneration, he will be much more prepared to speak about his mistakes and to look for reasonable solutions. In our case the boss offers the employee conversational therapy in which he can address the deep seated guilt he has about his daughter. In return, the employee agrees to remedy the mistakes in the industrial tents at his own expense (more precisely, by not charging the extra hours) and by personally apologizing to the customers.

The owner cannot simply let the matter rest. If he were to do so, he would do his other employees a disservice. Accusations *alone* could damage his company. The employee might, in light of his situation and his many years of reliability, view the accusations made to be ungrateful and exaggerated. He might then become demoralized and leave the company. In such a case further damage might befall the company via the loss of a good employee, and the employee would probably also not be helped personally by such actions.

4.5. To lead existentially means to be a personality and oneself

On the existential front it is natural that on the basis of personality certain things get weighted a bit differently. There are no two people who see each concrete situation completely similarly.

From the viewpoint of Christian ethics there is no unblemished decision which has absolutely nothing to do with the personality and personal history of the decision maker. With this reference to 'subjectivity' involved in every decision, the intention is not to deny every normative starting point and every situational weighing up of interests. Conversely, each decision, as basic and as firmly set upon values as it may be, is made by people who have their own personality, their own character, experiences, and previous history.

When addressing the subject of personality, this is not the place to trace the meaning and history of important concepts such as 'person' and 'personality.' It is from the ethicist Ulrich Eibach, who lives in Bonn, Germany and who holds the traditional view, that we want to borrow the fitting differentiation between person and personality.[179] Every person is a person because he was created in the image of God to be in relation to God and to his fellow man. Regardless of the condition in which an individual finds himself, be it as a child in the womb of his mother, as a coma patient or as a mentally handicapped person, everyone is endowed with personal dignity. In contrast, personality is that which this person does and says and brings to expression in interaction with other people. The dignity of a person lies in his personhood, not in his personality by which we get to know him. Still, it is the personality of each individual that differentiates people from each other and in which everything is brought to bear, including appearance, talents, abilities, knowledge, desires, character, experience, and goals.

God wants an unmistakable personality

Admittedly, many people have the same curious belief that religion and the church tend to restrict more than promote the development of personality. Does God, for instance, want to destroy our personality, our particular features, to flatten out our idiosyncrasies and to regiment our particular view of things? Does normative ethics possibly mean to no longer take one's

---

[179] Ulrich Eibach. Sterbehilfe – Tötung aus Mitleid: Euthanasie und 'lebensunwertes' Leben. R. Brockhaus: Wuppertal, 1998.

own personality and the personality of others into account? Something in this belief does not add up. According to the biblical witness it is God himself who has created us with distinctive personalities and who loves colossal diversity. He is the creator who via genetic order sees to it that no two people are truly the same. The following actually applies: the more that God frees us from our sinful behavior and frees us from addictions and dependencies, the more our unique personality comes to the fore. It is not for nothing that Christians are repeatedly called in the New Testament to serve with their particular talents and to not pursue a leveling down. Rather, the diversity of talents is to be enjoyed.

The destruction of personality is something that the Bible always associates with coercion. Coercion – all the way to obsession – is a mark of the devil. God does not work with coercion. The devil does not ask us, does not support us, does not help us, but rather he leads us to sin before we give thought. God, in contrast, gives us everything. He wants true personality that rules itself, and that sober-mindedly and imperturbably decides for the offer and way of God and takes this direction by the power of God.

The devil rules over people by robbing them of their personality, as is made clear in the healing of the Gerasene demoniac (Matthew 8:28-34; Mark 5:1-20; Luke 8:26-39). In this case a man had been completely robbed of his personality. He did not dress, and he lived in caves, spoke with no one, attacked people who came near (Mark 5:3-5; Luke 8:27, 29). Jesus' word of liberation brought about a return of his personality. The man ate normally, dressed himself, and spoke reasonably with others, which outsiders shockingly recognized (Mark 5:15: "When they came to Jesus, they saw the man who had been possessed by the legion of demons, sitting there, dressed and in his right mind; and they were afraid."; Luke 8: 35: "… and the people went out to see what had happened. When they came to Jesus, they found the man from whom the demons had gone out, sitting at Jesus' feet, dressed and in his right mind; and they were afraid").

Surely what we are looking at here is an extreme example – even within the New Testament – of the destruction of personality (not of the actual person and human dignity), and, correspondingly, the way to liberation via exorcism is the anomaly. This still clearly illustrates the following: God wishes to see the independently acting, unique personality in us come to the fore and where necessary to bring it forth again from underneath piled up layers.

The example of God's revelation in his Word via different personalities

The emergence of the Bible demonstrates very clearly that God treasures various personalities and uses them in his work. God did not just have his word fall from heaven or dictate it directly or have it written under coercion, which is the case with many mechanically inspired revelations in various religions but also found among Christian sects.[180] Where inspiration of a holy scripture is based on the idea that the human writers were completely will-less tools who wrote under coercion, one does not find a biblico-Christian understanding of inspiration. When God's Holy Spirit works through people, the Spirit makes these individuals into personalities and that also when composing his word. Paul considers it a given that prophets control themselves and revelation: "The spirits of prophets are subject to the control of prophets" (1 Corinthians 14:32). The Bible was not written mechanically by marionettes, but rather by characters whose uniqueness is expressed in their scriptures. Who would want to think that John's gospel could have just as easily been written by Paul and the Lamentations by King Solomon? Divine inspiration does not pass over human personality. Rather, it leads human personality to its complete unfolding.

It is for this reason that there is no religious book that propagates the purely human story of how it emerged and sees this as significant the way the Bible does. For example, in the Apostle Peter and the Apostle Paul we meet unique characters, whose life history, character, style and interests have hardly anything in common. Still, both their writings are found in the Bible. At the end of Peter's second letter, we even read the following: "… just as our dear brother Paul also wrote you with the wisdom that God gave him. He writes the same way in all his letters, speaking in them of these matters. His letters contain some things that are hard to understand, which ignorant and unstable people distort, as they do the other Scriptures, to their own destruction (2 Peter 3:15-16). The impulsive Peter, who seldom addresses topics elaborately, has difficulty to understand Paul's letters, since Paul seldom addresses a topic briefly. Still, for Peter there is no doubt that Paul is speaking in the name of God.

Jesus' life story is told in the New Testament by four different characters, in the four Gospels. The characters all have their own unique vantage points. This was not embarrassing for the early church. On the contrary, it was a valuable good that was worth passing on. There is no 'censored and unified history' of Jesus. Rather, the interests of the authors, whose character, experience, and interests had a say in the reports, are present.

---

[180] Comp. for example Christine und Thomas Schirrmacher. Mohammed: 'Prophet' aus der Wüste. Schwengeler: Berneck, 1987.³ pp. 37-39.

4. Deciding existentially

The meaning of experience for understanding God's revelation

An interesting chapter is the interlacing of the study of 'normative' Holy Scripture with our personality and experience. As desirous as it is to not read the Bible through the glasses of our own world views, it is unavoidable. I choose the example of the Holy Scripture due to the fact that if, in spite of its normative character, it cannot be read without our personality being involved, how much more so will this then apply for other sources relating to our ethical decisions.

In his book *The Doctrine of the Knowledge of God*, John M. Frame has pointed out that the biblical-theological perspective has normative, situational and existential sides.[181] In the Bible perception and knowledge are questions of the covenant relationship. For this reason the individual theologian plays a large role in the interpretation of the Bible for good or for bad.[182] On this account Arne Völkel aptly writes: "Only experienced individuals can conduct theology, and only experienced Christians can reflect theologically."[183]

For this reason we have to contend against the idea that we are so hopelessly determined by our culture, our experience, and our thinking that we only read our own thoughts out of the Bible. Along with this is contention against the view that any individual can understand the Bible completely so that what we read out of the Bible is just as binding for the world as is God's Word itself.

God desires that his word be authoritatively proclaimed and, at the same time, that we remain humble so as to be corrected by other Christians, by

---

[181] John M. Frame. The Doctrine of the Knowledge of God: A Theology of Lordship. Presbyterian & Reformed: Phillipsburg (NJ), 1987.

[182] Ibid., pp. 319-346, see also Bernhard Honsel. "Biographie und Theologie". Diakonia 17 (1986) 2: 77-84.

[183] Arne Völkel. Erfahrung als Voraussetzung theologischer Erkenntnis. Forum Christsein heute Nr. 76. Bundes Verlag: Witten, o. J. S. 4. In Völkel's work see particularly the following sections: "Erfahrung ist verarbeitendes Verstehen" (p. 4), "Leiderfahrung als Gotteserfahrung" (pp. 5-6); "Gehorsam als Gotteserfahrung" (pp. 6-7), und "Weisheit und Erfahrung" (p. 7). Regarding the importance of experience for theological work comp. further in Gerhard Ebeling. "Die Klage über das Erfahrungsdefizit der Theologie als Frage nach ihrer Sache." Wort und Glaube 3 (1975): 5-28; Gerhard Ruhbach. "Glaube und Erfahrung." pp. 93-99 in: Gerhard Ruhbach (ed.). Glaube, Erfahrung, Meditation. Kösel: München, 1977 and regarding the importance in the history of theology "Erfahrung," Parts III. and IV. (therein 1 and 2) pp. 109-131 in: Gerhard Krause, Gerhard Müller (ed.). Theologische Realenzyklopädie. Vol. X. Walter de Gruyter: Berlin, 1982; Martin Honecker. Einführung in die Theologische Ethik. Walter de Gruyter: Berlin, 1990. pp. 187-202.

the local believing community, and the entire church, and to never stop learning. The truly wise person recognizes that he has never learned everything and that that also applies to the study of the Holy Scriptures.

The fact alone that we have to translate the Bible and biblical teaching into our mother tongues means that our proclamation is tinted by us. That we can only study the Bible in light of our own knowledge and our own experience, although the Bible at the same time surpasses and changes our knowledge, is something that each Christian is aware of in interaction with the Bible on a daily basis as well as on Sunday.

Financial consultants in the same company are going to present to a young married couple expecting their first child differing recommendations from independent companies as to how to best provide financial security. A lot of what happens has to do with their own life history. A financial consultant who was the victim of an occupational accident will surely tend towards more conservative coverage that also takes the near future into account. An independent, young corporate consultant would tend more to look at the distant future (education of the children, provision for old age) and recommend more risky coverage. The recommendations presented by different consultants are not necessarily better or worse. What is bad, however, is if the consultants do not want to see how their own stories find a voice in what they present. A good financial consultant would himself offer a different consultant to assist, if he notices that his experience differs too greatly from that of the customers.

4.6. To lead existentially means to decide 'alone'

Even in the case where all the normative, situational and existential factors of a decision are taken into account, the most existential of all factors is the decision itself. In the final event, everyone has to completely personally decide 'in his heart' and for that reason take responsibility for his respective decision. No one can relieve him of the decision. Specifically in the case of a difficult balancing of interests it can become a lonely management decision. This can happen even where numerous discussions and consultations have taken place.

The final, internal decision that is made in front of our conscience is what really makes it a decision. Whatever has been deliberated and once stood under the condition that it could be reversed, is now irreversible. The decision becomes part of my existence and my personal history, for which I carry the full responsibility for better or for worse. This applies if the consequences are better than expected just as much as if they turn out worse than anticipated.

4. Deciding existentially

The most extreme example of a lonely decision is Jesus' decision to die on the cross for us (Luke 22:42-45). Immediately prior to being arrested, drenched with sweat, Jesus struggled with the question of death (Luke 22:44). The direction the decision would take was completely clear: "Father ... not my will, but yours be done" (Luke 22:42). Jesus came into the world for no other reason (Matthew 20:28) than to fulfill the will of his father – voluntarily. And still, it was at that moment that a normative and situational decision which had long been clear became an existential decision that shook Jesus' innermost being.

The Holy Scriptures want to keep up from playing the different aspects of ethics off against each other. Whoever only looks at the situational trade-off will end up canceling out every normative value. And whoever holds up only the normative aspects will not be able to give the word that brings resolution in many situations. An appeal to norms includes the existential acceptance of responsibility by conscience, just as conversely an appeal to conscience without any higher value was even possible for someone such as Adolf Hitler.

As Christians we have to consider the following with all decisions 1. Be conscious of our basic values and ordered reality, 2. Grasp situations and the possible consequences of our decisions as well as possible and assess them, and 3. Make a responsible decision which takes into account that the relationships between people are a valuable good.

For sure the comforting from James 1:5, "If any of you lacks wisdom, he should ask God, who gives generously to all without finding fault, and it will be given to him," can help us, especially when we face weighty decisions.

About the Author

Books by Thomas Schirrmacher in chronological order (With short commentaries)

As author:

Das Mißverständnis des Emil Brunner: Emil Brunners Bibliologie als Ursache für das Scheitern seiner Ekklesiologie. Theologische Untersuchungen zu Weltmission und Gemeindebau. ed. by Hans-Georg Wünch and Thomas Schirrmacher. Arbeitsgemeinschaft für Weltmission und Gemeindebau: Lörrach, 1982. 54 pp.

[The misunderstanding of Emil Brunner] A study and critique of Emil Brunner's ecclesiology and of the bibliology and hermeneutics of dialectical theology.

Mohammed: Prophet aus der Wüste. Schwengeler: Berneck (CH), 1984[1], 1986[2], 1990[3], 1996[4]. VTR: Nürnberg, 2006[5]. 120 pp.

[Muhammad] A short biography of the founder of Islam and an introduction into Islam.

Theodor Christlieb und seine Missionstheologie. Verlag der Evangelischen Gesellschaft für Deutschland: Wuppertal, 1985. 308 pp.

[Theodor Christlieb and his theology of mission] A study of the biography, theology and missiology of the leading German Pietist, professor of practical theology and international missions leader in the second half of the nineteenth century. (Thesis for Dr. theol. in missiology.)

Marxismus: Opium für das Volk? Schwengeler: Berneck (CH), 1990[1], 1997[2]. 150 pp.

[Marxism: Opiate for the People?] Marxism is proven to be a religion and an opiate for the masses. Empasizes the differences between Marxist and Biblical work ethics.

Zur marxistischen Sagen- und Märchenforschung und andere volkskundliche Beiträge. Verlag für Kultur und Wissenschaft: Bonn, 1991[1], 2003[2]. 227 pp.

[On the Marxist View of Sagas and Tales and other essays in folklore and culturalanthropology] 10 essays and articles on the science of folklore and cultural anthropology in Germany. Includes a critique of the Marxist interpretation of tales and sagas, and studies on the history of marriage and family in Europe from the 6th century onward.

„Der göttliche Volkstumsbegriff" und der „Glaube an Deutschlands Größe und heilige Sendung": Hans Naumann als Volkskundler und Germanist unter dem Nationalsozialismus. 2 volumes. Verlag für Kultur und Wissenschaft: Bonn, 2 volumes, 1992[1], in one volume 2000[2]. 606 pp.

[Hans Naumann as Anthropologist and Germanist under National Socialism] Discusses the history of German cultural anthropology and folklore under Hitler, especially the leading figure Naumann, professor of German language, whose scientific theory is shown to be very religious in tone. (Thesis for a PhD in Cultural Anthropology.)

War Paulus wirklich auf Malta? Hänssler: Neuhausen, 1992, VTR: Nürnberg, 2000[2] (together with Heinz Warnecke). 254 pp.

[Was Paul Really on Malta?] The book shows that Paul was not shipwrecked on Malta but on another island, Kephalenia, and that the report in Acts is very accurate. The Pauline authorship of the Pastoral Epistles is defended with theological and linguistic arguments against higher criticism.

Psychotherapie – der fatale Irrtum. Schwengeler: Berneck (CH), 1993[1], 1994[2]; 1997[3]; 2001[4] (together with Rudolf Antholzer). 150 pp.

[Psychotherapy – the Fatal Mistake] A critique of secular psychotherapy, showing that psychotherapy often is a religion, and that most psychotherapists call every school except their own to be unscientific.

Paulus im Kampf gegen den Schleier: Eine alternative Sicht von 1. Korinther 11,2-16. Biblia et symbiotica 4. Verlag für Kultur und Wissenschaft: Bonn, 1993[1], 1994[2], 1995[3], 1997[4] 168 pp. Revised: VTR: Nürnberg, 2002[5]

[Paul in Conflict with the Veil!?] *Exegetical examination of 1. Corinthians 11,2-16, following an alternative view of John Lightfoot, member of the Westminster assembly in the 16th century.*

"*Schirrmacher argues that from the biblical teaching that man is the head of woman (1 Cor 11:3) the Corinthians had drawn the false conclusions that in prayer a woman must be veiled (11:4-6) and a man is forbidden to be veiled (11:7), and that the wife exists for the husband but not the husband for the wife (11:8-9). Paul, however, rejected these conclusions and showed in 11:10-16 why the veiling of women did not belong to God's commandments binding upon all the Christian communities. After stating the thesis and presenting his alternative translation and exposition of 1 Cor 11:2-16, he considers the difficulties in the text, presents his alternative exposition in detail (in the form of thirteen theses), discusses quotations and irony in 1 Corinthians, and deals with other NT texts about women's clothing and prayer and about the subordination of wives.*" (New Testament Abstracts vol. 39 (1995) 1, p. 154).

Der Römerbrief. 2 vol. Neuhausen: Hänssler, 1994[1]; Hamburg: RVB & Nürnberg: VTR, 2001[2]. 331 + 323 pp.

[The Letter to the Romans] *Commentary on Romans in form of major topics of Systematic Theology starting from the text of Romans, but then going on to the whole Bible.*

Der Text des Römerbriefes: Für das Selbststudium gegliedert. Biblia et symbiotica 7. Verlag für Kultur und Wissenschaft: Bonn, 1994. 68 pp.

[The Text of the Letters to the Romans] *The text of Romans newly translated and structured for self study.*

Ethik. Neuhausen: Hänssler, 1994[1]. 2 vol. 883 & 889 pp.; Hamburg: RVB & Nürnberg: VTR, 2001[2]. 3 vol. 2150 pp.; 2002[3], 2009[4]; 2011[5]. 8 volumes. 2850 pp.

[Ethics] Major Evangelical ethics in German covering all aspects of general, special, persocial and public ethics.

Galilei-Legenden und andere Beiträge zu Schöpfungsforschung, Evolutionskritik und Chronologie der Kulturgeschichte 1979-1994. Biblia et symbiotica 12. Verlag für Kultur und Wissenschaft: Bonn, 1996. 331 pp.

[Legends of Galileo and other Contributions to Creation Science, Criticism of Evolution and Chronology of the History of Culture 1979-1994].

Völker – Drogen – Kannibalismus: Ethnologische und länderkundliche Beiträge 1984 – 1994. Verlag für Kultur und Wissenschaft: Bonn, 1997. 218 pp.

[Peoples – Drugs – Cannibalism] *A collection of articles on cultural anthropology, especially on Indians in South America, cannibalism and the religious use of drugs.*

Die Vielfalt biblischer Sprache: Über 100 alt- und neutestamentliche Stilarten,

Ausdrucksweisen, Redeweisen und Gliederungsformen. Verlag für Kultur und Wissenschaft: Bonn, 1997. 130 pp.

[The Diversity of Biblical Language] *A hermeneutical study, listing more than 100 specific language techniques in the Bible with several proof texts for each of them.*

Gottesdienst ist mehr: Plädoyer für einen liturgischen Gottesdienst. Verlag für Kultur und Wissenschaft: Bonn, 1998. 130 pp.

[Church Service is More] *An investigation into biblical proof texts for liturgical elements in Christian Sunday service.*

Gesetz und Geist: Eine alternative Sicht des Galaterbriefes. Reformatorische Paperbacks. Reformatorischer Verlag: Hamburg, 1999. 160 pp.

[Law and Spirit] *This commentary emphasising the ethical aspects of Galatians wants to prove that Galatians is not only fighting legalists but also a second party of Paul's opponents, who were totally opposed to the Old Testament and the Law, and lived immorally in the name of Christian freedom, a view especially endorsed by Wilhelm Lütgert's commentary of 1919. Paul is fighting against the abrogation of the Old Testament Law as well as against using this Law as way of salvation instead of God's grace.*

Law or Spirit? An Alternative View of Galatians. RVB International: Hamburg, 2001^1; 2008.^{2}. 160 pp.

English version of the same book.

God Wants You to Learn, Labour and Love. Reformation Books: Hamburg, 1999. 120 pp.

Four essays for Third World Christian Leaders on Learning with Jesus, Work Ethic, Love and Law and Social Involvement.

Dios Quiere que Tú Aprendas Trabajes y Ames. Funad: Managua (Nikaragua), 1999^1; 2000^2; RVB International: Hamburg, 2003^3. 70 pp.

[God Wants You to Learn, Labour and Love] Spanish version of the same book.

37 Gründe, warum Christen sich für eine Erneuerung unserer Gesellschaft auf christlicher Grundlage einsetzen sollten. Die Wende, 1999. 40 pp.

[37 reasons for Christian involvement in society and politics].

Christenverfolgung geht uns alle an: Auf dem Weg zu einer Theologie des Martyriums. Idea-Dokumentation 15/99. Idea: Wetzlar, 1999^1; 2001^2. 64 pp. New edition 2011^3: VKW

[The Persecution of Christians Concerns Us All: Towards a Theology of Martyrdom] *70 thesis on persecution and martyrdom, written for the International Day of Prayer for the Persecuted Church on behalf of the German and European Evangelical Alliance*

World Mission – Heart of Christianity. RVB International: Hamburg, 1999^1; 2008.^{2}. 120 pp.

Articles on the Biblical and systematic fundament of World Mission, especially on mission as rooted in God's being, on 'Mission in the OT', and 'Romans as a Charter for World Mission'. Shorter version of German original 2001.

Eugen Drewermann und der Buddhismus. Verlag für Theologie und Religionswissenschaft: Nürnberg, 2000^1; 2001^2. 132 pp.

[Drewermann and Buddhism] *Deals with the German Catholic Author Drewermann and his propagating Buddhist thinking. Includes chapter on a Christian Ethics of Environment.*

Ausverkaufte Würde? Der Pornographie-Boom und seine psychischen Folgen. Hänssler: Holzgerlingen, 2000. (with Christa Meves). 130 pp.

[The Selling Off of Dignity] *The psychological results of pornography.*

Eine Sekte wird evangelisch – Die Reformation der Weltweiten Kirche Gottes.

Idea-Dokumentation 11/2000. Idea: Wetzlar, 2000. 56 pp.

[A Cult Becomes Protestant] *Detailed report on the reformation of the Worldwide Church of God (Herbert W. Armstrong) from a sect to an evangelical church.*

Legends About the Galilei-Affair. RVB International: Hamburg, 2001[1]; 2008.[2]. 120 pp.

Shorter version of the German book 'Galilei-Legenden' mentioned above with essays on the Galilei-affair and creation science.

Human Rights Threatened in Europe: Euthanasia – Abortion – Bioethicconvention. RVB International: Hamburg, 2001[1]; 2008.[2]. 100 pp.

Updated Lectures on euthanasia and biomedicine at the 1st European Right to Life Forum Berlin, 1998, and articles on abortion.

Menschenrechte in Europa in Gefahr. RVB: Hamburg, 2001... 110 pp.

[Human Rights Threatened in Europe] *Updated Lectures on euthanasia and biomedicine at the 1st European Right to Life Forum Berlin, 1998, and articles on abortion. See slightly different English version above.*

Aufbruch zur modernen Weltmission: William Careys Theologie. RVB. 64 pp.

[Be Keen to Get Going: William Careys Theology] *First discussion of Carey's theology in length, explaining his Calvinistic and Postmillenial backround.*

Be Keen to Get Going: William Careys Theology. RVB: Hamburg, 2001[1]; 2008.[2]. 64 pp.

Same book in English.

Darf ein Christ schwören? RVB: Hamburg, 2001. 140 pp.

[May Christians Take an Oath?] *On Swearing and on its meaning for covenant theology. Taken from 'Ethik', vol. 1.*

Christus im Alten Testament. RVB: Hamburg, 2001. 84 pp.

[Christ in the Old Testament] *On Christ and the Trinity in the Old Testament and on 'the Angel of the Lord'. Taken from 'Ethik'.*

Wie erkenne ich den Willen Gottes? Führungsmystik auf dem Prüfstand. RVB: Hamburg, 2001. 184 pp.

[How to know the will of God] – *Critizeses the inner leading of the Spirit. Taken from 'Ethik'.*

Love is the Fulfillment of Love – Essays in Ethics. RVB: Hamburg, 2001[1]; 2008.[2]. 140 pp.

Essays on ethical topics, including role of the Law, work ethics, and European Union.

Mission und der Kampf um die Menschenrechte. RVB: Hamburg, 2001. 108 S.

[Mission and the Battle for Human Rights] *The relationship of world missions and the fight for human rights is discussed on an ethical level (theology of human rights) as well as on a practical level.*

The Persecution of Christians Concerns Us All: Towards a Theology of Martyrdom. At the same time Idea-Dokumentation 15/99 E. VKW: Bonn, 2001. 156 pp.

70 thesis on persecution and martyrdom, written for the International Day of Prayer for the Persecuted Church on behalf of the German and European Evangelical Alliance

Irrtumslosigkeit der Schrift oder Hermeneutik der Demut? VTR: Nürnberg, 2001. 82 pp.

[Inerrancy of Scripture or 'Hermeneutics of Humility'] *Debate with Dr. Hempelmann on the inerrancy of scripture.*

Beiträge zur Kirchen- und Theologiegeschichte: Heiligenverehrung — Universität Gießen — Reformation / Augustin – Böhl — Spurgeon — Brunner. VKW: Bonn, 2001. 200 pp.

[Essay on the History of church and Dogma] *Articles on topics from church history like 'The beginning of the veneration of saints' and on the named theologians.*

Weltmission — Das Herz des christlichen Glaubens: Beiträge aus 'Evangelikale Missiologie'. VKW: Bonn, 2001. 200 pp.

[World Mission – Heart of Christianity] *Articles on the Biblical and systematic fundament of World Mission, especially on mission as rooted in God's being, on 'Mission in the OT', and 'Romans as a Charter for World Mission.. Shorter version of German original 2001.*

Säkulare Religionen: Aufsätze zum religiösen Charakter von Nationalsozialismus und Kommunismus. VKW: Bonn, 2001. 140 pp.

[Secular Religions] *Articles on the religious nature of National Socialism and Communism. Includes texts of prayers to Hitler.*

Paulus im Kampf gegen den Schleier!? VTR: Nürnberg, 2002[5]. 130 pp.

Revised version. See commentary on first edition 1993[1].

Paul in Conflict with the Veil!? VTR: Nürnberg, 2002[1]; 2007[2]. 130 pp.

Same book in English.

Hoffnung für Europa: 66 Thesen. VTR: Nürnberg, 2002

Official thesis and study of hope in the Old and New Testament for Hope for Europe of the European Ev. Alliance and Lausanne Europe.

Hope for Europe: 66 Theses. VTR: Nürnberg, 2002

Same book in English.

Also available in Czech, Dutch, Spanish, Rumanian, Portuguese, French, Russian, Italian, Hungarian, Latvian.

ABC der Demut. RVB: Hamburg, 2002

[ABC of Humility] *Notes and bible studies on humility in alphabetical order.*

Führen in ethischer Verantwortung: Die drei Seiten jeder Verantwortung. Edition ACF. Brunnen: Gießen, 2002

[Leading in ethical responsibility] *An introduction into ethcis for economic and other leaders for the Academy of Christian Leaders.*

Der Papst und das Leiden: Warum der Papst nicht zurücktritt. VTR: Nürnberg, 2002. 64 pp.

[The Pope and Suffering] *A study of the writings of Pope John II. on suffering and an evaluation of their exegetical basis. Gives reasons why the pope does not resign.*

Erziehung, Bildung, Schule. VTR: Nürnberg, 2002. 88 pp.

[Instruction, Education, School] *The chapters on rising of children, example, education, and Christian school from 'Ethics'.*

Thomas Schirrmacher, Christine Schirrmacher u. a. Harenberg Lexikon der Religionen. Harenberg Verlag: Düsseldorf, 2002. 1020 pp.

[Harenberg Dictionary of World Religions] *In a major secular dictionary on world religions, Thomas Schirrmacher wrote the section on Christianity ('Lexicon of Christianity', pp. 8-267) and Christine Schirrmacher the section on Islam ('Lexicon of Islam', 'pp. 428-549).*

Studies in Church Leadership: New Testament Church Structure – Paul and His Coworkers – An Alternative Theological Education – A Critique of Catholic Canon Law. VKW: Bonn, 2003[1]; RVB: Hamburg, 2008.[2]. 112 pp.

Contains the named five essays. The first essay is translated from vol. 5 of 'Ethics'.

Im Gespräch mit dem Wanderprediger des New Age – und andere apologetische Beiträge. VKW: Bonn, 2003. 210 pp.

[In Discussion with the Itinerant Preacher of the New Age] *Essays and reports on non-Christian religions, New Age,* reincarnation, manicheism from two decades of apologetic debates.

Verborgene Zahlenwerte in der Bibel? – und andere Beiträge zur Bibel. VKW: Bonn, 2003. 200 pp.

[Secret Numbers in the Bible?] Essays and articles on Bible Numerics, the importance of Hebrew studies, Obadiah, the Psalms and other Bible related topics from 2 decades of studies.

Feindbild Islam. VKW: Bonn, 2003. 111 pp.

[Bogeyman Islam] *May Arab Christians call God ‚Allah'? Is Allah the Father of Jesus? How Politcal Parties in Germany misrepresant Islam.*

Religijos mokslas. Prizmês knyga. Siaulai (Litauen): Campus Fidus, 2004. 106 pp.

[Secular Religions] In Latvian: Essays on Religions, Marxism, National Socialism and the devil in Art and Literature.

Bildungspflicht statt Schulzwang. VKW/VTR/idea: Bonn et. al., 2005. 90 pp.

[Compulsary Education or Compulsary Schooling] *A scientific evaluation of homeschooling.*

Der Ablass RVB/VTR: Hamburg, 2005. 144 pp.

[The Indulgences] History and theology of the Catholic view on indulgences.

Die Apokryphen RVB/VTR: Hamburg, 2005. 92 pp.

[The Apocrypha] *History and theology of the Catholic view on the apocrypha and an apology of the Protestant position.*

Scham- oder Schuldgefühl? Die christliche Botschaft angesichts von schuld- und schamorientierten Gewissen und Kulturen. Verlag für Kultur und Wissenschaft: Bonn, 2005. 99 pp.

[Shame- and Guiltfeeling] *This study explains the difference between shame- and guiltoriented cultures and shows, that the 'Biblical' message emphasizes shame and guilt equally and thus can be applied to cultures in the West, the East, in modern and in Third World cultures.*

Thomas Schirrmacher et al. Christ und Politk: 50 Antworten auf Fragen und kritische Einwände. VKW: Bonn, 2006. 125 pp.

[Christians and Politics] *Schirrmacher and three members of parliament from Switzerland answer questions around the relation of church and state and the political involvement of Evangelicals.*

Der Segen von Ehe und Familie: Interessante Erkenntnisse aus Forschung und Statistik. VKW: Bonn, 2006. 125 pp.

[The Blessing of Marriage and Family] Introduction to 200 scientific studies and statistics, that prove the blessing of longterm marriage and stable family.

Multikulturelle Gesellschaft: Chancen und Gefahren. Hänssler: Holzgerlingen, 2006. 100 pp.

[Multicultural Society] A history of multiculturalism (especially Muslims and Russian-Germans) in Germany and its political, economic and religious implications for the future of Germany.

Die neue Unterschicht: Armut in Deutschland? Hänssler: Holzgerlingen, 2007. 120 pp.

[The New Low Cast] A sociology of low cast people in Germany, the differences in culture to low cast people one hundred years ago, tasks for churches and the State.

Hitlers Kriegsreligion: Die Verankerung der Weltanschauung Hitlers in seiner religiösen Begrifflichkeit und seinem Gottesbild. 2 vol. VKW: Bonn, 2007. 1220 pp.

[Hitlers Religion of War] *A research about the religious terms and thoughts in all texts and speeches of Hitler of Hitler, pleading for a new way of explaining Hitlers worldview, rise and breakdown.*

About the Author

Moderne Väter: Weder Waschlappen, noch Despot. Hänssler: Holzgerlingen, 2007. 96 pp.

[Modern Fathers] Presents the result of international father research, explains the necessity of the father's involvement for his children and gives practical guidelines.

Sheria au Roho? Trans-Africa Swahili Christian Ministries: Mwanza, Tanzania, 2007.[1]; 2008.[2]; 2010.[3]; 2011.[4]. 96 pp.

Kiswahili-Version of 'Law and Spirit' about Galatians.

Mateso ya Wakristo Yanatuhusu Sisi Sote: Kuelekea Theolojia ya Mashahidi wa Imani. Trans-Africa Swahili Christian Ministries: Mwanza, Tanzania, 2008.[1]; 2010.[2;] 2011.[3]

Kiswahili-Version of 'The Persecution of Christians Concerns Us All'

Upendo ni Utimilifu wa Sheria: Insha juu ya Maadili. Trans-Africa Swahili Christian Ministries: Mwanza, Tanzania, 2008.[1]; 2010.[2]; 2011.[3]

Kiswahili-Version of 'Love is the Fulfillment of Law'.

Koran und Bibel: Die größten Religionen im Vergleich. Hänssler: Holzgerlingen, 2008. 96 pp.

[Quran and Bible] *Compares the differences between the Muslim of the Quran as the 'Word of God' and the Christian view of the Bible as the 'Word of God'. A classic on the inspiration of the Bible.*

Christenverfolgung heute. Hänssler: Holzgerlingen, 2008. 96 pp.

[The Persecution of Christians today] *Gives an overview over the persecution of Christians worldwide and presents a short theology of persecution as well political reasons for the fight for religious freedom.*

Internetpornografie. Hänssler: Holzgerlingen, 2008. 156 pp.

[Internet pornography] *Intense study of spread of pornography, its use amongst children and young people, its psychological results and dangers, including steps how to escape sex and pornography addiction.*

Prawda o pornografii. Translated by I. W. Proswirjakowoj. Moskau: Wjatka, 2009. 170 pp.

Prawda o pornografii. Bonn: VKW, 2010. 170 pp.

Russian Edition of 'Internet pornography'.

May a Christian Go to Court and other Essays on Persecution vs. Religious Freedom. WEA Global Issues Series. VKW: Bonn, 2008. 120 pp.

Essays: "Is Involvement in the Fight Against the Persecution of Christians Solely for the Benefit of Christians?", "But with gentleness and respect: Why missions should be ruled by ethics". "May a Christian Go to Court?", "Putting Rumors to Rest", "Human Rights and Christian Faith", "There Has to Be a Social Ethic".

Rassismus: Alte Vorurteile und neue Einsichten. Hänssler: Holzgerlingen, 2009. 120 pp.

[Racism] *History and scientific errors of racism*

Fundamentalismus: Wenn Religion gefährlich wird. SCM Hänssler: Holzgerlingen, 2010. 120 pp.

[Fundamentalism] *History of term, definition, examples from all religions.*

Menschenhandel: Die Rückkehr der Sklaverei. SCM Hänssler: Holzgerlingen, 2011. 106 pp.

[Human Trafficking: The Return of Slavery] *History and present situation of human trafficking including Europe, discusses legal and other reasons that prevent the fight against modern slavery.*

Responsabilitatea etica in luarea deciziilor (2011) Scriptum, Oradea (Romania), 2011. 210 pp.

Rumanian version of 'Führen in ethischer Verantwortung' (2002).

Demnitate pierduta - Pornografia pe internet. Adevaruri, pericole, evolutie. Oradea (Romania): Scriptum, 2011. 208 pp.
Rumanian version of 'Internetpornography'.

Indulgences: A History of Theology and Reality of Indulgences and Purgatory. VKW: Bonn, 2011. 164 pp.
History and theology of the Catholic view on indulgences.

Thomas Schirrmacher, Richard Howell. Racism. With an essay on Caste in India. VKW: Bonn, 2011. 100 pp.
History and scientific errors of racism

Missio Dei: Mission aus dem Wesen Gottes. Komplementäre Dogmatik Reihe 2. Hamburg, Nürnberg, 2011. 100 pp.

[Missio Dei: Mission as an Attribute of God] *The trinitarian foundations of mission and missiology with three chapters: historical, exegetical and ecumenical studies (especially on the dividing 'filioque'-discussion).*

Mungu Akutaka Ujifunze, Ufanye Kazi na Upende. Trans-Africa Swahili Christian Ministries: Mwanza, Tanzania & RVB International: Hamburg, 2011. 100 pp.
Kiswahili-Version of 'God wants you to learn ... '.

Tumaini Kwa Afrika: Hoja 66. Trans-Africa Swahili Christian Ministries: Mwanza, Tanzania & RVB International: Hamburg, 2011. 100 pp.

[Hope for Africa: 66 Thesis"]

Mafunzo Yahusuyo Uogozi wa Kanisa. Trans-Africa Swahili Christian Ministries: Mwanza, Tanzania & RVB International: Hamburg, 2012. 120 pp.
Kiswahili-Version of 'Studies in Church Leadership'.

Menschenrechte: Anspruch und Wirklichkeit. Holzgerlingen: SCM Hänssler, 2012. 120 pp.

[Human Rights]: *Ethical arguments for human rights versus the present stage of the violation of human rights worldwide.*

Christ and the Trinity in the Old Testament. Edited by James E. Anderson. RVB: Hamburg, 2013. 82 pp.

In the process of publishing:

Human Trafficking

Leadership an Ethical Responsibility

Fundamentalism: When Religion becomes Dangerous

Culture of Shame / Culture of Guilt

Advocate of Love – Martin Bucer as Theologian and Pastor

The Koran and the Bible

(Ed.) William Carey: Theologian – Linguist – Social Reformer

Unterdrückte Frauen (with Christine Schirrmacher) [Supressed Women: A Global Perspectives]

Schwangerschaftsabbruch (with Ute Buth) [Abortion: A Guidebook]

As editor (always with own contributions):

Patrick Johnstone. Handbuch für Weltmission: Gebet für die Welt. Hänssler: Neuhausen, 1987[2], newest edition 1993[6] (together with Christine Schirrmacher). 811 pp.

[Handbook on World Mission] *Adapted German version of 'Operation World', a handbook and lexicon on the situation of Christianity and missions in every country of the world.*

Gospel Recordings Language List: Liste der Sprachaufnahmen in 4.273 Sprachen. Missiologica Evangelica 4. Verlag für Kultur und Wissenschaft: Bonn, 1992. 120 pp.
List of 4273 languages in the world, in which evangelistic cassettes are available.

„Die Zeit für die Bekehrung der Welt ist reif": Rufus Anderson und die Selbständigkeit der Kirche als Ziel der Mission. Edition afem: mission scripts 3. Verlag für Kultur und Wissenschaft: Bonn, 1993. 134 pp.

[The Time of Conversion is Ripe: Rufus Anderson and The Independence of ...] *Articles by Schirrmacher and by theologians from the 19th century about Rufus Anderson, leading American missionary statesman, Reformed professor of missions and postmillennial theologian – together with the first translation of texts of Anderson into German.*

William Carey. Eine Untersuchung über die Verpflichtung der Christen [1792]. Edition afem: mission classics 1. Verlag für Kultur und Wissenschaft: Bonn, 1993 (together with Klaus Fiedler). 100 pp.

[An Inquire into the Means ...] *First German translation of the book by the Calvinist Baptist William Carey of 1792, with which the age of modern Protestant world missions started.*

Bibeltreue in der Offensive: Die drei Chicagoerklärungen zur biblischen Unfehlbarkeit, Hermeneutik und Anwendung. Biblia et symbiotica 2. Verlag für Kultur und Wissenschaft: Bonn, 1993[1]; 2005[2,] 2009[3]. 132 pp.

German translation of the three Chicago-Declarations on biblical inerrancy, hermeneutics and application.

Im Kampf um die Bibel – 100 Jahre Bibelbund. Biblia et symbiotica 6. Verlag für Kultur und Wissenschaft: Bonn, 1994 (together with Stephan Holthaus). 168 pp.

[The Battle for the Bible] *'Festschrift' for 100 years of "Bibelbund". Articles on biblical inerrancy and on the history of the major German organization fighting higher criticism, the "Bibelbund" (Bible League), and its theological journal "Bibel und Gemeinde", edited by Schirrmacher 1988-1997.*

Eduard Böhl. Dogmatik. Hänssler Theologie. Hänssler: Neuhausen, 1995; 2nd ed.: Hamburg: RVB & Bonn: VKW, 2004. 508 pp.

[Dogmatic Theology] *A Reformed Systematic Theology from the last century edited by Thomas Schirrmacher; with an lengthy introduction on Böhl's life and work.*

Der evangelische Glaube kompakt: Ein Arbeitsbuch. Hänssler: Neuhausen, 1998; 2nd ed.: Hamburg: RVB & Bonn: VKW, 2004. 246 pp.

[The Protestant Faith in Nuce] *German translation of the Westminster Confession of Faith, adapted and with commentary and changes in Presbyterian, Congregationalist and Baptist versions.*

Werden alle gerettet? Referate der Jahrestagung 1998 des AfeM (with Klaus W. Müller). Verlag für Kultur und Wissenschaft: Bonn, 1998. 160 pp.

[Will All Be Saved?] *The proceedings of a missiological consultation on the relationship between Christianity's mission and other religions.*

The Right to Life for Every Person / Lebensrecht für jeden Menschen. Abortion – Euthanasia – Gen Technology: Proceedings of the 1st European Right to Life Forum Berlin, 1998. Abtreibung – Euthanasie – Gentechnik: Beiträge des 1. Europäischen Forums Lebensrecht Berlin, 1999 (with Walter Schrader, Hartmut Steeb). Verlag für Kultur und Wissenschaft: Bonn, 1999. 310 pp.

Basic articles on biomedical topics, includes reports on the prolife movements in most European countries.

Kein anderer Name: Die Einzigartigkeit Jesu Christi und das Gespräch mit nichtchristlichen Religionen. Festschrift zum 70. Geburtstag von Peter Beyerhaus. Verlag für Theologie und Religionswissenschaft: Nürnberg, 1999. 470 pp.

[No Other Name: The Uniqueness of Jesus Christ ...] *Festschrift for Prof. Peter Beyerhaus, the leading evangelical authority on missions, ecumenical issues and on other religions and an evangelical elder statesmen. Covers all aspects of the relationship of Christian faith to other religions.*

Missionswissenschaft im Zeichen der Erneuerung: Ehrengabe zum 70. Geburtstag von Peter Beyerhaus. Sonderausgabe = Evangelikale Missiologie 15 (1999) Heft 2 (together with Klaus W. Müller und Christof Sauer) (1999) afem

Shorter version of the former Festschrift for mass distribution

Ausbildung als missionarischer Auftrag: Referate der Jahrestagung 1999 des AfeM (with Klaus W. Müller). Verlag für Kultur und Wissenschaft: Bonn, 2000. 210 pp.

[Theological education as World Mission] Lectures on the relation of missions and theological education by leading representatives of theological schools, alternative programmes, missions and third world churches.

Mission in der Spannung zwischen Hoffnung, Resignation und Endzeitenthusiasmus: Referate der Jahrestagung 2000 des AfeM (together with Klaus W. Müller). Verlag für Kultur und Wissenschaft: Bonn, 2001. 240 pp.

Lectures on the relation of eschatology and missions in history and in present reality.

Märtyrer 2001 — Christenverfolgung vor allem in islamischen Ländern. (with Max Klingberg). VKW: Bonn, 2001. 140 pp.

[Martyrs 2001] Documentation on the present status of persecution of Christians in Islamic countries.

Anwalt der Liebe – Martin Bucer als Theologe und Seelsorger: Zum 450. Todestag des Reformators. Jahrbuch des Martin Bucer Seminars 1 (2001). VKW: Bonn, 2001. 160 pp.

[Advocate of Love: Martin Bucer as Theologian and Counselor] Yearbook of the Martin Bucer Seminary on Life and Theology of the reformer Martin Bucer.

Die vier Schöpfungsordnungen Gottes: Kirche, Staat, Wirtschaft und Familie bei Dietrich Bonhoeffer und Martin Luther. VTR: Nürnberg, 2001. 110 pp.

[The four Creation Orders] Three lengthy essays discuss the importance of the four major creation orders family, church, work and state in the Bible, and in the work of Martin Luther and Dietrich Bonhoeffer.

Baumeister bleibt der Herr: Festgabe zum 80. Geburtstag von Prof. Bernd Schirrmacher (with Klaus Schirrmacher und Ingrid von Torklus). VKW: Bonn, 2001. 33300 pp.

[God Stays the Master Builder] Festschrift for Thomas Schirrmacher's father on his 80th birthday. Essays mainly concentrate on Christian education and Evangelical schools.

A Life of Transformation: Festschrift for Colonel V. Doner. RVB International: Hamburg, 2001. 350 pp.

Festschrift for one of the giants of international Christian relief work and social involvement.

Märtyrer 2002 — Jahrbuch zur Christenverfolgung heute (with Max Klingberg). VKW: Bonn, 2002. 140 pp.

[Martyrs 2002] Yearbook with documentation of the present status of persecution of Christians with special emphasize on Indonesia, Pakistan, Turkey and Vietnam.

Patrick Johnstone. Gebet für die Welt. Hänssler: Holzgerlingen, 2003. 1010 pp.

[Prayer for the World] Adapted German version of 'Operation World', a handbook and lexicon on the situation of Christianity and missions in every country of the world.

Märtyrer 2003 — Jahrbuch zur Christenverfolgung heute (with Max Klingberg). VKKW: Bonn, 2003. 180 pp.

[Martyrs 2003] Yearbook with documentation of the present status of persecu-

tion of Christians, featuring Cuba, Japan, North Korea, Vietnam.

Wenn Kinder zu Hause zur Schule gehen (with Thomas Mayer). VTR: Nürnberg, 2004. 260 pp.

[When Children Go to Scholl at Home] *Documentation and scientific essays on homeschooling in Germany and Europe.*

Menschenrechte für Minderheiten in Deutschland und Europa: Vom Einsatz für die Religionsfreiheit durch die Evangelische Allianz und die Freikirchen im 19. Jahrhundert (with Karl Heinz Voigt). Verlag für Kultur und Wissenschaft: Bonn, 2004. 120 pp.

[Human Rights for Minorities in Germany and Europe] *Research articles on the history of the defence of religious freedom by the Evangelical Alliance in Germany and Great Britain in the 19th century.*

Herausforderung China: Ansichten, Einsichten, Aussichten: Eine Dokumentation von idea und China Partner (with Konrad Brandt). Verlag für Kultur und Wissenschaft: Bonn, 2004. 214 pp.

[Challenge China] A collection of reports, lectures and opinion on the situation of religions and the Christian faith in China, combining reports on persecution and reports on huge progress for public Christianity.

Europa Hoffnung geben: Dokumentation (with Thomas Mayer). VTR: Nürnberg, 2004. 197 pp.

[To Give Hope to Europe] Lectures of a theological conference in Budapest by John-Warwick Montgomery, Thomas K. Johnstone, William Mikler, Bernhard Knieß on the future of Europe and how to defend the gospel of hope in Europe.

Märtyrer 2004 – Das Jahrbuch zur Christenverfolgung heute. (with Max Klingberg). VKW: Bonn, 2004. 160 pp.

[Martyrs 2004] *Yearbook with documentation of the present status of persecution of Christians, with two longer studies on the situation in Nigeria and Iran.*

Tabuthema Tod? Vom Sterben in Würde. (with Roland Jung, Frank Koppelin). Jahrbuch des Martin Bucer Seminars 4 (2004). VKW: Bonn, 2004. 220 pp.

[Death as Taboo?] 8 major Evangelical ethicists discuss topics around counseling serious ill and dying people, death, euthanasia, counseling to relatives.

Mission verändert – Mission verändert sich / Mission Transformes – Mission is Transformed: Festschrift für Klaus Fiedler. (with Christof Sauer). Nürnberg: VTR & Bonn: VKW, 2005. 572 pp.

Festschrift for African missionary and doyen of African and German mission history Klaus Fiedler.

Märtyrer 2005 – Das Jahrbuch zur Christenverfolgung heute. (mit Max Klingberg). VKW: Bonn, 2005. 170 pp.

[Martyrs 2005] *Yearbook with documentation of the present status of persecution of Christians, featuring Nigeria, China, Indonesia, Vietnam, Turkey.*

Ein Maulkorb für Christen? Juristen nehmen Stellung zum deutschen Antidiskriminierungsgesetz und ähnlichen Gesetzen in Europa und Australien. (with Thomas Zimmermanns). VKW: Bonn, 2005

[A Muzzle for Christians?] *Studies in religious hate laws, antidiscrimination laws and their influence on Christian communities.*

Scham- und Schuldorientierung in der Diskussion: Kulturanthropologische, missiologische und theologische Einsichten (mit Klaus W. Müller). VTR: Nürnberg & VKW: Bonn, 2006

[Shame- and Guiltorientation] *A selection of experts from all continents on the difference between shame- and guiltoriented cultures and its implications for world missions.*

Familienplanung – eine Option für Christen? . Verlag für Kultur und Wissenschaft: Bonn, 2006. 170 pp.
[Family Planing – An Option for Christians?] *A Protestant view of family planing.*

Märtyrer 2006 – Das Jahrbuch zur Christenverfolgung heute. (with Max Klingberg und Ron Kubsch). VKW: Bonn, 2006. 170 pp.
[Martyrs 2006] *Yearbook with documentation of the present status of persecution of Christians, concentrating on Iran, Iraq, Turkey and North Korea.*

Martin Bucer als Vorreiter der Mission. VKW: Bonn & VTR: Nürnberg, 2006. 110 pp.
[Martin Bucer as Forunner of World Mission] Essays from the 19th century to the present on Martin Bucer being the only Reformator arguing in favour of world mission.

Märtyrer 2007 – Das Jahrbuch zur Christenverfolgung heute. (with Max Klingberg und Ron Kubsch). VKW: Bonn, 2007. 200 pp.
[Martyrs 2007] *Yearbook with documentation of the present status of persecution of Christians, concentrating on India, Turkey, Iraq, Indonesia and Germany.*

HIV und AIDS als christliche Herausforderung 1: Grundsätzliche Erwägungen. (mit Kurt Bangert). Verlag für Kultur und Wissenschaft: Bonn, 2008. 211 pp.
[HIV and AIDS as Christian Challenge 1: General Discussion] *Essay on how the Christian church should react to HIV and AIDS and how it does react. Published together with World Vision Germany.*

HIV und AIDS als christliche Herausforderung 2: Aus der praktischen Arbeit. (mit Kurt Bangert). Verlag für Kultur und Wissenschaft: Bonn, 2008. 280 pp.

[HIV and AIDS as Christian Challenge 2: What Is Done and Can Be Done] *Volume 2 of the same*

Märtyrer 2008 – Das Jahrbuch zur Christenverfolgung heute. (with Max Klingberg und Ron Kubsch). VKW: Bonn, 2008. 180 pp.
[Martyrs 2008] *Yearbook with documentation of the present status of persecution of Christians, concentrating on Iran, Egypt, Afghanistan, Germany, Vietnam, Turkey.*

Johannes Calvin. Christliche Glaubenslehre: Erstausgabe der 'Institutio' von 1536. VKW: Bonn, 2008
New German edition of the first edition of John Calvins Institutes (1536) with lengthy introduction.

Märtyrer 2009 – Das Jahrbuch zur Christenverfolgung heute. (with Max Klingberg und Ron Kubsch). VKW: Bonn, 2009. 270 pp.
[Martyrs 2009] *Yearbook with documentation of the present status of persecution of Christians, concentrating on India, Eritrea, Yemen.*

Glaube nur im Kämmerlein? Zum Schutz religiöser Freiheitsrechte konvertierter Asylbewerber. (with Friedemann Burkhardt). VKW/Idea: Bonn, 2009. 100 pp.
[Faith only in the Chamber?] *The protection of religious freedom rights for asylum seekers in Germany having converted from Islam to Christianity.*

Die Aufnahme verfolgter Christen aus dem Irak in Deutschland: Die Vorgeschichte eines ungewöhnlichen Beschlusses im Spiegel der Presse. VKW/Idea: Bonn, 2009. 130 pp.
[The entry of persecuted Christians from Iraq into Germany] *Press articles during 2008 documenting the decision of the German government and the EU to accept thousands of Christians refugees from Iraq.*

Der Kampf gegen die weltweite Armut – Aufgabe der Evangelischen Allianz? Zur biblisch-theologischen Begründung der Micha-Initiative. (with Andreas Kusch). VKW/Idea: Bonn, 2009. 230 pp.

[The fight against poverty – task of the Evangelical Alliance?] *Essays by theologians, missiologists, activists etc. in favour of the MICAH initiative of the World Evangelical Alliance.*

Tough-Minded Christianity: Honoring the Legacy of John Warwick Montgomery. (with William Dembski). (2009) B&H Academic Publ.: Nashville (TN). 830 pp.

Large Festschrift with essays by many major Evangelical theologians and lawyers.

Calvin and World Mission: Essays- VKW: Bonn, VTR: Nürnberg, 2009. 204 pp.

Collection of essays from 1882 to 2002.

Märtyrer 2010 – Das Jahrbuch zur Christenverfolgung heute. (with Max Klingberg und Ron Kubsch). VKW: Bonn, 2010. 200 pp.

[Martyrs 2010] *Yearbook with documentation of the present status of persecution of Christians, concentrating on China, India, Nigeria, Indonesia, and the German parliament and Catholic martyrology.*

Märtyrer 2011 – Das Jahrbuch zur Christenverfolgung heute. (with Max Klingberg und Ron Kubsch). VKW: Bonn, 2011. 300 pp.

[Martyrs 2011] *Yearbook with documentation of the present status of persecution of Christians, concentrating on the Arab World, Egypt, Eritrea, Nigeria, China and Europe.*

Märtyrer 2012 – Das Jahrbuch zur Christenverfolgung heute. (with Max Klingberg und Ron Kubsch). VKW: Bonn, 2012. 300 pp.

[Martyrs 2012] *Yearbook with documentation of the present status of persecution of Christians, concentrating on the Nigeria, India, Indonesia, and on the sharia.*

Der Islam als historische, politische und theologische Herausforderung (mit Christine Schirrmacher). VKW: Bonn, 2013. 186 pp.

[Islam as a historic, political and theological challenge] *Yearbook of the Martin Bucer European school of Theology and Research Institutes – Essays from seven scholars.*

Gott – der Drei-Eine: Anstoß der Mission. (with Robert Badenberg, Friedemann Knödler). VKW: Bonn, 2012. 170 pp.

[Gott – The Triune: Origian of Mission] *Plenaries and workshops of a consultation on the relationship of the doctrine of trinity to postmodern approaches to reach the Muslim world.*

Biography

Prof. Dr. theol. Dr. phil. Thomas Schirrmacher, PhD, DD, (born 1960) is Ambassador for Human Rights of the World Evangelical Alliance, speaking for appr. 600 million Christians, chair of its Theological Commission, and director of its International Institute for Religious Freedom (Bonn, Cape Town, Colombo). He is also director of the Commission for Religious Freedom of the German and Austrian Evangelical Alliance. He is member of the board of the International Society for Human Rights.

Schirrmacher is professor of the sociology of religion at the State University of the West in Timisoara (Romania) and Distinguished Professor of Global Ethics and International Development at William Carey University in Shillong (Meghalaya, India). He is also president of 'Martin Bucer European Theological Seminary and Research Institutes' with small campuses in Bonn, Berlin, Zurich, Linz, Innsbruck, Prague, Istanbul, and Sao Paulo, where he teaches ethics and comparative religions.

He studied theology from 1978 to 1982 at STH Basel (Switzerland) and since 1983 Cultural Anthropology and Comparative Religions at Bonn State University. He earned a Drs. theol. in Missiology and Ecumenics at Theological University (Kampen/Netherlands) in 1984, and a Dr. theol. in Missiology and Ecumenics at Johannes Calvin Foundation (Kampen/Netherlands) in 1985, a Ph.D. in Cultural Anthropology at Pacific Western University in Los Angeles (CA) in 1989, a Th.D. in Ethics at Whitefield Theological Seminary in Lakeland (FL) in 1996, and a Dr. phil. in Comparative Religions / Sociology of Religion at State University of Bonn in 2007. In 1997 he received an honorary doctorate (D.D.) from Cranmer Theological House, in 2006 one from Acts University in Bangalore.

Schirrmacher regularly testifies in the German parliament and other parliaments in Europe, in the EU parliament in Brussels, the OSCE in Vienna and the UN Human Rights Council in Geneva.

His newest books are on human rights (2012), human trafficking (2011), fundamentalism (2010), racism (2009), and in German only: persecution of Christians in Iraq (2009), HIV/AIDS as Christian challenge (2008), internet pornography (2008), and Hitler's religion of war (2007). His 92 books were published in 17 languages.

He is listed in Marquis' Who's Who in the World, Dictionary of International Biography, International Who is Who of Professionals, 2000 Outstanding Intellectuals of the 21st Century and many other biographical yearbooks.

World Evangelical Alliance

World Evangelical Alliance is a global ministry working with local churches around the world to join in common concern to live and proclaim the Good News of Jesus in their communities. WEA is a network of churches in 129 nations that have each formed an evangelical alliance and over 100 international organizations joining together to give a worldwide identity, voice and platform to more than 600 million evangelical Christians. Seeking holiness, justice and renewal at every level of society – individual, family, community and culture, God is glorified and the nations of the earth are forever transformed.

Christians from ten countries met in London in 1846 for the purpose of launching, in their own words, "a new thing in church history, a definite organization for the expression of unity amongst Christian individuals belonging to different churches." This was the beginning of a vision that was fulfilled in 1951 when believers from 21 countries officially formed the World Evangelical Fellowship. Today, 150 years after the London gathering, WEA is a dynamic global structure for unity and action that embraces 600 million evangelicals in 129 countries. It is a unity based on the historic Christian faith expressed in the evangelical tradition. And it looks to the future with vision to accomplish God's purposes in discipling the nations for Jesus Christ.

Commissions:

- Theology
- Missions
- Religious Liberty
- Women's Concerns
- Youth
- Information Technology

Initiatives and Activities

- Ambassador for Human Rights
- Ambassador for Refugees
- Creation Care Task Force
- Global Generosity Network
- International Institute for Religious Freedom
- International Institute for Islamic Studies
- Leadership Institute
- Micah Challenge
- Global Human Trafficking Task Force
- Peace and Reconciliation Initiative
- UN-Team

Church Street Station
P.O. Box 3402
New York, NY 10008-3402
Phone +[1] 212 233 3046
Fax +[1] 646-957-9218
www.worldea.org

International Institute for Religious Freedom

Purpose and Aim

The "International Institute for Religious Freedom" (IIRF) is a network of professors, researchers, academics, specialists and university institutions from all continents with the aim of working towards:

- The establishment of reliable facts on the restriction of religious freedom worldwide.
- The making available of results of such research to other researchers, politicians, advocates, as well as the media.
- The introduction of the subject of religious freedom into academic research and curricula.
- The backing up of advocacy for victims of violations of religious freedom in the religious, legal and political world.
- Serving discriminated and persecuted believers and academics wherever they are located. Publications and other research will be made available as economically and as readily available as possible to be affordable in the Global South.

Tools

The IIRF encourages all activities that contribute to the understanding of religious freedom. These include:

- Dissemination of existing literature, information about archives, compilation of bibliographies etc.
- Production and dissemination of new papers, journals and books.
- Gathering and analysis of statistics and evidence.
- Supplying of ideas and materials to universities and institutions of theological education to encourage the inclusion of religious freedom issues into curricula.
- Guiding postgraduate students in research projects either personally or in cooperation with the universities and educational institutions.
- Representation at key events where opportunity is given to strengthen connections with the wider religious liberty community and with politicians, diplomats and media.

Online / Contact:

- www.iirf.eu / info@iirf.eu

IIRF

International Institute for Religious Freedom
Internationales Institut für Religionsfreiheit
Institut international pour la liber té religieuse
of the World Evangelical Alliance
Bonn – Cape Town – Colombo

Friedrichstr. 38	PO Box 535	32, Ebenezer Place
2nd Floor	Edgemead 7407	Dehiwela
53111 Bonn	Cape Town	(Colombo)
Germany	South Africa	Sri Lanka

Board of Supervisors
- *Chairman:* **Godfrey Yogarajah** (Sri Lanka)
- *Chairman emeritus:* Dr. Paul C. Murdoch
- Esme Bowers (South Africa)
- Julia Doxat-Purser (European Evangelical Alliance)
- John Langlois (World Evangelical Alliance)

Executives
- *Director:* **Prof. Dr. Dr. Thomas Schirrmacher** (Germany)
- *Co-Director:* **Prof. Dr. Christof Sauer** (South Africa)
- *Director Colombo Office:* **Roshini Wickremesinhe**, LLB (Sri Lanka)
- *CFO:* Manfred Feldmann (Germany)
- *Legal Counsel:* Martin Schweiger (Singapore)
- *Representative to UN, OSCE, EU:* Arie de Pater (Netherlands)
- *Senior research writer:* Fernando Perez (India)
- *Research Coordinator:* Joseph Yakubu (Nigeria)
- *Public relations:* Ron Kubsch (Germany)

Academic Board
with areas of research
- *Honorary Chairman:*
  Prof. Dr. Dr. John Warwick Montgomery (France)
- Tehmina Arora, LLB (India):
  Anti-conversion laws
- Prof. Dr. Janet Epp Buckingham (Canada):
  Human rights law
- Dr. Rosalee Velosso Ewell (Brazil):
  Consultations
- Prof. Dr. Lovell Fernandez (South Africa):
  Transitional justice
- Prof. Dr. Ken Gnanakan (India):
  Universities, Social justice
- Dr. Benyamin Intan (Indonesia):
  Peacebuilding
- Prof. Dr. Thomas Johnson (Czech Republic):
  Natural law ethics
- Max Klingberg (Germany):
  Human rights organizations
- Drs. Behnan Konutgan (Turkey):
  Orthodox Churches
- Dr. Paul Marshall (USA):
  Religious liberty research, Islam
- Patson Netha (Zimbabwe): Africa
- Ihsan Yinal Özbek (Turkey): Turkish Islam
- Prof. Glenn Penner † (Canada)
- Prof. Dr. Bernhard J. G. Reitsma (Netherlands): Islam and Christianity
- Prof. Dr. Christine Schirrmacher (Germany):
  Islamic Sharia
- Prof. Dr. Donald L. Stults (USA): Training
- Anneta Vyssotskaia (Russia):
  Central and Eastern Europe

The institute operates under the oversight of the World Evangelical Alliance and is registered as a company in Guernsey with its registered office at PO Box 265, Suite 6, Borough House, Rue du Pré, Saint Peter Port, Guernsey, Channel Islands, GY1 3QU.

The Colombo Bureau is registered with the Asia Evangelical Alliance, Sri Lanka.
The Cape Town Bureau is registered as 'IIRF Cape Town Bureau' in South Africa.
The Bonn Bureau is registered under ProMundis e. V. (Bonn, 20 AR 197/95)

Institute of Islamic Studies

The protestant "Institute of Islamic Studies" is a network of scholars in Islamic studies and is carried out by the Evangelical Alliance in Germany, Austria and Switzerland.

Churches, the political arena, and society at large are provided foundational information relating to the topic of 'Islam' through research and the presentation thereof via publications, adult education seminars, and democratic political discourse.

Research Focus

As far as our work is concerned, the focus is primarily on Islam in Europe, the global development of Islamic theology and of Islamic fundamentalism, as well as a respectful and issue-related meeting of Christians and Muslims. In the process, misunderstandings about Islam and Muslims can be cleared up, and problematic developments in Islamic fundamentalism and political Islam are explained. Through our work we want to contribute to engaging Muslims in an informed and fair manner.

What we do

Lectures, seminars, and conferences for public authorities, churches, political audiences, and society at large

- Participation in special conferences on the topic of Islam
- The publication of books in German, English, and Spanish
- The preparation of scholarly studies for the general public
- Special publications on current topics
- Production of a German-English journal entitled "Islam and Christianity"
- Regular press releases with commentaries on current events from a scholarly Islamic studies perspective
- Academic surveys and experts' reports for advisory boards of government
- Regular news provided as summaries of Turkish and Arab language internet publications
- Fatwa archive
- Website with a collection of articles

Islam and Christianity

Journal of the Institute of Islamic Studies and the International Institute of Islamic Studies

- German/English. All articles in both languages
- Topics of current issues: Women in Islam, Human Rights in Islam, Sharia law, Shii Islam.
- Editor: Prof. Dr. Christine Schirrmacher
  Executive Editor: Carsten Polanz
- ISSN 1616-8917
- 48 pp. twice annually
- 9,20 € per year including postage (airmail on request)
- **Sample copies and subscription**:
  Ifl · Pf 7427 · D-53074 Bonn · Germany
  info@islaminstitut.de
- **Download** under www.islaminstitut.de/zeitschrift.20.0.html

Institute for Islamic Studies (Ifl)
of the Evangelical Alliance in Germany, Austria, Switzerland

International Institute of Islamic Studies (IIIS)
of the World Evangelical Alliance

Ifl · Pf 7427 · D-53074 Bonn · Germany · info@islaminstitut.de

www.islaminstitute.net

International Institute
of Islamic Studies

Giving Hands

GIVING HANDS GERMANY (GH) was established in 1995 and is officially recognized as a nonprofit foreign aid organization. It is an international operating charity that – up to now – has been supporting projects in about 40 countries on four continents. In particular we care for orphans and street children. Our major focus is on Africa and Central America. GIVING HANDS always mainly provides assistance for self-help and furthers human rights thinking.

The charity itself is not bound to any church, but on the spot we are co-operating with churches of all denominations. Naturally we also cooperate with other charities as well as governmental organizations to provide assistance as effective as possible under the given circumstances.

The work of GIVING HANDS GERMANY is controlled by a supervisory board. Members of this board are Manfred Feldmann, Colonel V. Doner and Kathleen McCall. Dr. Christine Schirrmacher is registered as legal manager of GIVING HANDS at the local district court. The local office and work of the charity are coordinated by Rev. Horst J. Kreie as executive manager. Dr. theol. Thomas Schirrmacher serves as a special consultant for all projects.

Thanks to our international contacts companies and organizations from many countries time and again provide containers with gifts in kind which we send to the different destinations where these goods help to satisfy elementary needs. This statutory purpose is put into practice by granting nutrition, clothing, education, construction and maintenance of training centers at home and abroad, construction of wells and operation of water treatment systems, guidance for self-help and transportation of goods and gifts to areas and countries where needy people live.

GIVING HANDS has a publishing arm under the leadership of Titus Vogt, that publishes human rights and other books in English, Spanish, Swahili and other languages.

These aims are aspired to the glory of the Lord according to the basic Christian principles put down in the Holy Bible.

Baumschulallee 3a • D-53115 Bonn • Germany
Phone: +49 / 228 / 695531 • Fax +49 / 228 / 695532
www.gebende-haende.de • info@gebende-haende.de

Martin Bucer Seminary

Faithful to biblical truth
Cooperating with the Evangelical Alliance
Reformed

Solid training for the Kingdom of God
- Alternative theological education
- Study while serving a church or working another job
- Enables students to remain in their own churches
- Encourages independent thinking
- Learning from the growth of the universal church.

Academic
- For the Bachelor's degree: 180 Bologna-Credits
- For the Master's degree: 120 additional Credits
- Both old and new teaching methods: All day seminars, independent study, term papers, etc.

Our Orientation:
- Complete trust in the reliability of the Bible
- Building on reformation theology
- Based on the confession of the German Evangelical Alliance
- Open for innovations in the Kingdom of God

Our Emphasis:
- The Bible
- Ethics and Basic Theology
- Missions
- The Church

Our Style:
- Innovative
- Relevant to society
- International
- Research oriented
- Interdisciplinary

Structure
- 15 study centers in 7 countries with local partners
- 5 research institutes
- President: Prof. Dr. Thomas Schirrmacher
  Vice President: Prof. Dr. Thomas K. Johnson
- Deans: Thomas Kinker, Th.D.;
  Titus Vogt, lic. theol., Carsten Friedrich, M.Th.

Missions through research
- Institute for Religious Freedom
- Institute for Islamic Studies
- Institute for Life and Family Studies
- Institute for Crisis, Dying, and Grief Counseling
- Institute for Pastoral Care

www.bucer.eu • info@bucer.eu
Berlin I Bielefeld I Bonn I Chemnitz I Hamburg I Munich I Pforzheim
Innsbruck I Istanbul I Izmir I Linz I Prague I São Paulo I Tirana I Zurich